The Good Sales Manager's Guide

Over 80 practical checklists for day-to-day selling and sales management

Tom Cannon

METO
Russell Square House
10-12 Russell Square
London WC1B 5BZ

Telephone: 020 7872 9000
Facsimile: 020 7872 9099
Website: http://www.meto.org.uk
E-mail: enquiries_meto@csi.com

METO is the National Training Organisation for Management and
Enterprise.

ISBN 1 897587 45 7

Acknowledgements

My thanks go to my colleagues at METO Emma Harris and Robert
Stein whose suggestions and editorial advice were invaluable.

Project management by Genesys Editorial Limited

Printed and bound in Great Britain by Ashford Colour Press

Typeset by Leech Design

Preface

Selling is the lifeblood of business. Without the sale (or other form of completed transaction such as a lease or hire) of a good or service no other aspect of the enterprise can be sustained. More people are employed in sales (face-to-face, telesales, electronic and other forms) than any other profession.

The skilled salesperson works with transactions that range from the sale of a simple good or service at a local retail outlet to the complex international transaction that can take years to complete and involve vast financing and complex technologies.

Sometimes selling is a personal or individual activity, but selling increasingly involves the management of teams to get the maximum effect.

The range of these challenges places increasing pressure on skilled sales personnel and their managers to get the best from their own efforts and those of their colleagues. This requires a constant effort to up-grade skills and achieve world class standards of performance.

Contents

Preface   iii

How to use this guide   vii

Getting the best from the customer base and winning new customers   I

The opportunity   3

The market   9

Improving performance   15

Research   17

Sales planning   25

Customer support   35

Communication   37

Getting to yes   47

Conclude the sale   51

Tenders, key accounts and major projects   55

Evaluate the offer to tender   57

Replying to the tender   59

Presenting to key accounts   63

Co-ordinating the project team   69

Presenting the product or service   79

Demonstration   81

Order processing and delivery   85

After sales support and service   89

Pricing 103

Proposed price 105

Financing 109

Part exchange 117

Contributing to the marketing effort 121

The marketing effort 123

Innovation 127

Managing yourself and others 131

Improving your own performance 133

Developing teams 137

Glossary 141

Appendix 1 National Standards 147

What are National Standards? 148

National Vocational Qualifications 149

The NVQ Process 150

The Sales Standards 151

Appendix 2 Useful contacts 173

Index 175

The sales manager's role is increasingly complex and challenging. Good sales managers are expected to lead in the selling process, manage their teams, tackle increasingly diverse customer groups, use new technologies and contribute to the wider marketing and business goals of the business. They need to react to fast changing conditions and increasing competition.

The *Good Sales Manager's Guide* breaks down selling and the sales manager's role into simple, practical checklists to help you and your colleagues tackle successfully the novel as well as the everyday tasks. There is no magic, just clear guidelines based on good practice presented in plain language.

Use the checklists for everyday guidance, your own development and that of your colleagues. There is a six-step way to use the guide as a training tool, as follows.

1. Ask yourself the question: What are the new selling and sales management tasks you will be facing over the next six to twelve months?
2. Ask yourself: What are the five most important and urgent sales and sales management issues you will face over the next six to twelve months?
3. Use the contents pages of this book to identify the checklists that fit your needs.
4. Plan and organise your training and development to give you the additional knowledge, skill and experience to conduct these activities effectively.
5. Undertake this training to help you carry out the tasks identified in the checklists, monitor and review your progress.
6. Assess your performance – using the checklists – and get others to give you feedback.

If you complete these steps successfully, you could qualify for the new Sales or Sales Management National Vocational Qualifications or Scottish Vocational Qualifications. Refer to Appendix 1 for details.

CHAPTER 1

Getting the best from the customer base and winning new customers

The opportunity

This section is about making the best use of your organisation's selling ability by assessing its products, services and its customer base.

The checklists will help you to

■ gather the relevant information on products and services and evaluate their success

■ decide what criteria to use when selling to your customers

■ look for potential outside your existing customer base

■ create a strategy for the development of your customer base.

1 | Evaluate existing products and services

- ❑ Keep accurate records on enquiries, sales, returns and complaints.

- ❑ Evaluate existing products and services for their ongoing contribution to the organisation.

- ❑ Gather information regularly about who the existing products and services are being sold to.

- ❑ Seek feedback about existing products and services from customers and sales staff.

- ❑ Assess and analyse feedback against other available information from inside and outside the organisation.

- ❑ Produce an overall profile of products and services and present this picture and your conclusions to the appropriate people.

- ❑ Ensure that recommendations for changes in the product and service range are made in the correct format to the appropriate people.

Determine the organisation's criteria for selling to customers   2

❑ Ensure that information is regularly gathered about what customers currently buy.

❑ Review existing criteria for selecting target customers according to organisational guidelines.

❑ Establish which sales targeting and marketing criteria best fit the organisation's product and service range.

❑ Estimate the potential effect on sales of a change in criteria.

❑ Ensure that any recommendations for changes to the criteria used to select and target customers to improve performance are presented in the correct format to the appropriate people.

3 | Assess the potential for expansion in the existing customer base

❑ Gather and evaluate information that may be of use in assessing potential expansion.

❑ Identify the information that is most useful for assessing potential expansion.

❑ Produce and update continuously lists of currently available products and services, and also of those that may be available in the future.

❑ Study and analyse the buying patterns and profiles of different customers for their potential to inform the expansion of the product and service range.

❑ Invite customers to supply information regularly about their anticipated future needs and interests.

❑ Seek suggestions of ways in which it may be possible to expand the product and service range and ensure that these, and your proposals, are made to the appropriate people.

Assess the potential for attracting new customers

4

❑ Gather information about the sorts of customers who are likely to buy the organisation's products and services.

❑ Review other sources of information about potential customers, identify potential customers and ensure that relevant information is obtained.

❑ Review and assess past performance of the organisation in attracting new customers.

❑ Identify, review and assess different methods of, and approaches to, contacting new customers who may be appropriate to the organisation.

❑ Make decisions on which new methods of attracting customers should be used and ensure that these methods are implemented on a trial basis.

❑ Review and identify the customer profiles most likely to be attracted to the organisation's product and service range.

5 | Develop an overall sales strategy for developing the customer base

❑ Gather information about customers from a variety of reliable internal and external sources and analyse data for its impact on the development of the customer base.

❑ Make decisions on the key aspects of the sales strategy which relate to the development of the customer base.

❑ Allocate budgets to facilitate the implementation of the chosen strategy for developing the customer base.

❑ Accurately calculate timescales in order to establish when the initial investment in customers should be recovered. Consider using simple breakeven analysis.

❑ Decide on the amount of freedom sales staff will have to offer discounts, special deals, trade-in values and other terms of sale.

❑ Develop, establish and introduce a system to monitor the progress of the sales strategy, and identify the performance indicators to be used.

❑ Prepare and present sales strategy to the appropriate people, in order to influence future sales planning and effective implementation.

The market

This section is about how to identify potential customers and how best to approach them and your current customers about your organisation's products and services.

The checklists will help you to

■ find ways to identify who the potential customers are

■ make the first contact with customers and use it to full advantage

■ inform the customer about the benefits of your products and services.

6 Identify potential customers, influencers and decision makers within current and potential customers

❑ Identify business contacts and use these and other contacts to make introductions to potential customers.

❑ Identify by name, assess, and map where possible, the roles of those who influence purchase decisions and decision makers within customer organisations.

❑ Establish the level of influence and buying power of individuals.

❑ Evaluate changes in the customer's personnel for the potential impact on business opportunities and relationships.

❑ Share information about the role of individuals within customer organisations with the relevant people inside and outside the organisation.

❑ Ensure that all contact with customers is conducted in a manner aimed at generating goodwill and promoting the objectives of the organisation.

❑ Maintain all contact with customers within the organisation's accepted protocols and ethical limits, and conform to appropriate legal requirements.

Make initial contact with potential customers to interest them in products and services 7

❏ Select the most appropriate methods for contacting different customers.

❏ Contact the person who is able to make buying decisions.

❏ Clearly identify and confirm the customer's interest in particular products and services.

❏ Ensure that the customer is aware of the range of relevant products and services and the terms at which they can be supplied.

❏ Actively pursue opportunities to promote further contact to interest the customer in buying the organisation's products and services.

❏ Maintain clear records of contact with customers and any further action that is required.

❏ Promptly pass and accurately record information about customers, their buying needs and any further action that is required to pursue sales to the appropriate people.

❏ Inform appropriate people of unfruitful leads or contacts.

8A Advise customers and potential customers of the range and benefits of the organisation's products and services

❑ Note and clarify the reasons why customers are interested in particular products and services.

❑ Clearly present to the customer the relevant features and benefits of products and services.

❑ Provide satisfactory answers to the customer's queries, satisfy their objections or provide alternative strategies.

❑ Supply the customer with full details about the terms of sale that can be offered and the ways in which products and services can be packaged.

❑ Ensure that sufficient information is gathered from the customer to prepare proposals or formal presentations about products and services.

❑ Gather relevant information about other suppliers who may be competing for business from the customer.

❑ Conduct contact with customers in a manner that promotes goodwill and a positive image of the organisation.

Advise customers and potential customers of the range and benefits of the organisation's products and services

❑ Establish the benefits the customer requires from the products and services in which they are interested.

❑ Identify and prepare relevant and useful information about the organisation's products and services.

❑ Choose the most appropriate way of communicating information to customers.

❑ Supply accurate information to the customer about the organisation's products and services.

❑ Emphasise to the customer the features and benefits of the organisation's products and services.

❑ Ensure that, where appropriate, further activity to progress sales is agreed with the customer.

❑ Answer clearly and accurately the customer's queries or objections and respond to customer enquiries in a manner which promotes the organisation and its products and services.

❑ Consult relevant colleagues where the customer's request for information or clarification of points of interest are outside own remit or level of knowledge and understanding.

CHAPTER 2

Improving performance

→ Research

This section is about the identification of measurable and achievable objectives concerning your sales performance and ways for you to achieve them.

The checklists will help you to

■ use relevant information to develop sales forecasts for products

■ measure your performance and the performance of colleagues

■ look for ways to improve sales performances by the use of objectives

■ use and improve customer networks to help reach objectives.

9 | Analyse sales of products and services

❏ Gather, analyse and use relevant and up-to-date information in order to forecast sales potential.

❏ Analyse and assess past sales performance.

❏ Analyse trends and market conditions to indicate the future pattern of sales.

❏ Identify and assess factors affecting sales trends, market conditions and potential selling opportunities.

❏ Evaluate previous sales figures and relevant trends.

❏ Use sales figures and trend data to build forecasts of the market and personal potential.

❏ Complete sales forecasts and record them according to organisational guidelines.

(See also checklist 15 on page 26)

Monitor and evaluate individual sales calls and own sales performance

10

- ❏ Measure objectives met and not met during sales calls against targets and own personal sales plan.

- ❏ Recognise, note and correct errors or shortcomings in personal performance during sales calls.

- ❏ Take action to promote improvement in performance where errors or shortcomings in personal performance are identified.

- ❏ Take action to reinforce and build upon recognised, effective personal performance and work to identify and overcome weaknesses.

- ❏ Seek evaluation by others of personal performance and act upon their advice.

- ❏ Identify problems in achieving call objectives, which are outside of own control, review these for validity and, where necessary, refer to an appropriate authority, if possible.

11 Agree and achieve objectives for improving sales performance

❏ Assess personal sales performance using information from sales figures and personal objectives.

❏ Seek and respond positively to views of others on personal sales performance and agree objectives for improving performance.

❏ Identify, analyse, and use the under-achievement, achievement or over-achievement of forecasts and objectives by self and others to improve future practice and development planning.

❏ Agree methods for learning and adapting behaviour in the light of past performance with relevant people.

❏ Follow learning plans and assess progress towards meeting development objectives. Review conclusion with the relevant people and take appropriate action.

❏ Highlight important lessons learnt, or particular learning methods that are beneficial. Discuss these with the appropriate people to inform future practice.

❏ Use analysis of sales information to provide a clear evaluation of the reasons why objectives are, or are not, being achieved. Supply evaluations and recommendations in the required format to all relevant people when needed.

❏ Make recommendations for adjustments to sales objectives based on the analysis of sales information, supported by a clear rationale.

Develop networks across the current and prospective customer base

- ❏ Set up accurate, reliable and sustainable systems to keep contact with existing customers and identify potential customers.

- ❏ Map current networks of customers and potential clients.

- ❏ Identify and contact a sample of customers to discuss and spell out in detail the networks to which they belong.

- ❏ Select the methods which are going to be used to develop networks of customers and support groups.

- ❏ Use existing networks in order to gain contact with customers.

- ❏ Where possible use existing customers to endorse or contact these wider networks.

- ❏ Formalise networks to encourage customers to keep in contact with the organisation.

13	**Audit customer networks to determine opportunities for improvement, expansion and re-orientation**

❏ Assess the extent to which network activities have contributed to sales.

❏ Tactfully question samples of customers about their membership of networks and their use of these networks.

❏ Identify the most effective networks especially from user groups, interest groups and social groups.

❏ Specify and list networks and networking activities by order of their value in sales and leads.

❏ Increase contacts with effective networks and seek ways to increase the returns from less effective networks or abandon their use.

Extend customer networks to provide a base for improved sales | 14

- ❑ Ensure that new customers are informed about networks and invited to participate.

- ❑ Define and describe the benefits of joining networks to new members in order to encourage them to participate.

- ❑ Build new customer networks into wider personal and company networks.

- ❑ Discuss and record benefits sought and obtained by new customers and new network members.

- ❑ Encourage other staff to join networks.

Sales planning

This section is about the procedures to follow when developing and implementing plans and strategies for sales.

The checklists will help you to

- evaluate information to prepare forecasts for sales
- create a sales plan that will achieve the targets set
- research and analyse information to identify trends and developments in the market and evaluate the success of sales plans and sales targets
- make suggestions about both the development and improvement of the sales strategy.

| 15 | **Forecast sales of products and services** |

❑ Obtain and analyse sales and market information to identify trends in sales and draw out the market conditions that could show a future pattern of sales.

❑ Note, investigate and assess any new factors and trends that might affect future sales and establish what impact they are likely to have.

❑ Evaluate any previous forecasts to see how far they have been achieved, and identify the reasons for achievement and under-achievement.

❑ Set and agree sales forecasts with everyone involved.

❑ Seek and consider seriously suggestions about how the forecast can be achieved and exceeded.

❑ Confirm with all staff the new forecasts, and work to encourage those involved to meet and exceed them.

(See also checklist 9 on page 18)

Develop and implement a sales plan to achieve targets

16

- ❑ Clearly define the objectives of the sales plan and make sure they are in line with the organisation's sales objectives.

- ❑ Make sure that the content of the plan is based upon the organisation's sales objectives, identified market conditions and up-to-date customer information.

- ❑ Break down the sales plan to produce individual targets and objectives.

- ❑ Specify within the sales plan how agreed sales targets are to be realistically achieved.

- ❑ Present the sales plan in the required format and communicate it in a manner which helps others understand its objectives and content.

- ❑ Ensure that milestones and review processes are specified in the plan.

- ❑ Consult all appropriate people in the design of the plan and fully brief them on their roles and when the plan is to be implemented.

- ❑ Identify all relevant sales activities for meeting the objectives of the plan, discuss the activities with the appropriate people and detail the programme of work within the plan.

- ❑ Specify and detail team and individual activity within the plan.

- ❑ Make certain that the resources necessary to implement the sales plan are identified and are in place.

17 | Identify trends, developments and current market conditions

❑ Research and identify the most relevant and significant trends and developments affecting the organisation.

❑ Identify valid sources of information such as: commercial databases, in-house databases, cuttings services, market intelligence services, trade press, specialised journals about the chosen trends, developments and market conditions.

❑ Establish and put in place systems to monitor trends, developments and market conditions and brief the appropriate people on their use.

❑ Monitor information gained through monitoring systems, and note any trends, developments and market conditions which appear to be important.

❑ Assess and identify important trends, developments and market conditions, draw out their potential significance and pass the results of the analysis to the relevant people.

Monitor and evaluate sales plans   18

❑ Review the sales plan according to the agreed review schedule and where circumstances require.

❑ Monitor, and assess carefully, progress towards meeting the plan's objectives.

❑ Review the success of the chosen sales activities regularly throughout the duration of the plan and amend the activities where necessary.

❑ Note, and assess for their likely impact on the plan's success, all likely problems in achieving the plan's objectives or implementing the plan's methods.

❑ Prepare contingency plans, and put them into place where problems with the plan's implementation or shortfalls in its achievement are identified.

❑ Invite all relevant people to provide input into the review of the plan and any contingency plans which are produced.

❑ Brief all relevant people on the success of the plan and invite them to provide feedback.

❑ Note successes and failures and use them to inform future practice.

19 Monitor, analyse and evaluate the achievement of sales targets

❑ Set up information systems to identify the progress that is being made towards the achievement of sales targets.

❑ Regularly review the information obtained from the systems, monitor the value of the data and highlight areas where objectives have been met, where there are shortfalls, and where targets have been exceeded.

❑ Analyse the information obtained from the systems to identify the factors that lead to different levels of achievement.

❑ Investigate factors that appear to lead to under-achievement. Prepare and introduce methods and approaches that will reduce them.

❑ Study factors that lead to exceeding targets and use findings to change sales methods and approaches.

❑ Compare sales with previous sales figures and the sales of competitors. Use a variety of means to undertake this comparison, ensuring that like-with-like comparisons are used and that factors such as inflation are taken into account.

❑ Produce a sales analysis to show how far sales meet the targets set.

❑ Summarise the analysis and pass it on to the appropriate people.

Gather, analyse and evaluate the sales activities of the organisation and its competitors

❑ Identify the best methods for gathering information about competitors.

❑ Create and put in place systems, or employ existing ones, to monitor the sales activities of the organisation and its competitors, and brief appropriate people on their use.

❑ Collate and check to confirm that such systems produce valid and reliable information about the sales activities of the organisation and its competitors.

❑ Ensure that valid methods are used for analysing information about the sales activities of the organisation and its competitors, and that these methods make it possible to compare different factors.

❑ Undertake evaluations comparing the sales activities of the organisation and its competitors, while being certain that these evaluations are complete, accurate and contain all relevant details.

❑ Accurately summarise evaluations of the sales activities of the organisation and its competitors and pass these assessments on to relevant people.

21 | Contribute to the development and implementation of sales strategy

❑ Gather and organise, in a useful format, valid information which will help develop sales strategy.

❑ Evaluate information to help develop sales strategy and identify significant issues which will have an impact on the strategy.

❑ Ensure that information to help develop a sales strategy is based on a realistic analysis of market opportunities and contributes to the setting of clear objectives for the organisation.

❑ Identify, consult and prepare for their role the staff who will be responsible for implementing different aspects of sales strategy.

❑ Define the criteria of success of the sales strategy, ensure they are applied, and create systems to monitor its success.

❑ Execute developments and changes that will help support sales strategy.

Recommend changes to improve sales strategy | 22

❑ Regularly evaluate information about performance and the achievement of sales strategy.

❑ Analyse important changes and developments in the market for their potential impact on the sales strategy.

❑ Evaluate activities and resources commissioned to support the sales strategy for their success in promoting the strategy.

❑ Ensure sales tactics are consistent with strategy.

❑ Assess developments in the market against the organisation's resource capability to determine the organisation's ability to respond to the developments and remain competitive.

❑ Accurately estimate the cost and resource implications of introducing changes to sales strategy.

❑ Make certain that recommendations for changes to sales strategy contain relevant details about the anticipated benefits of implementing them.

❑ Present recommendations for changes to sales strategy in an agreed format to appropriate stakeholders.

CHAPTER 3

Customer support

Communication

This section is about how to communicate successfully when dealing with your customers to improve working relationships and achieve sales.

The checklists will help you to

■ improve your working relationships with customers

■ look at how to support the customers' needs

■ use different types of communication depending on the customer concerned

■ use your personal image to its best advantage

■ tell when it is possible to try to up sell or cross sell

■ get customers interested in products and services

■ prepare for sales negotiations

■ arrange any follow up calls to potential customers.

23 | Develop and enhance positive working relationships with customers

❏ Deal with all customers in a manner that enhances trust and goodwill towards self and the organisation.

❏ Conduct all contact with customers within accepted protocols and ethics while complying with legal requirements.

❏ Explain clearly and accurately to the customer organisational and legal limits of responsibility and authority.

❏ Pursue opportunities for improving working relationships with customers.

❏ Take all possible actions to minimise conflict between the customer's needs and organisational limitations.

❏ Accurately record contact with customers where necessary.

❏ Refer customers to colleagues who are qualified to advise them, where information or advice is outside of own remit of responsibility.

❏ Resolve difficulties in working with clients where possible, or discuss with an appropriate authority.

Customer support   24

- ❏ Make determined attempts to meet customer needs within own limits of authority.
- ❏ Explain limits on organisation clearly and positively to the customer.
- ❏ Ensure that all possible actions are taken to minimise conflict between customer needs and organisational limitations.
- ❏ Identify organisational limitations, explore their implications for performance, discuss and seek assistance from others where necessary.
- ❏ Record clearly proposals to customers, and store in the appropriate place.

25 | Adapt methods of communication to the customer

❏ Ensure that appropriate types of communication are selected to keep customers informed about current or future actions.

❏ Adapt written and spoken language to the customer.

❏ Ensure that methods of communication are suited to customers with individual needs.

❏ Check understanding of communication regularly with customer.

❏ Openly acknowledge and seek appropriate help with any communication difficulties.

Present positive personal image to customer 26

❑ Ensure that treatment of customers is always courteous and helpful, especially when working under pressure.

❑ Consistently maintain organisational standards for personal appearance and behaviour.

❑ Make certain that equipment and supplies used in transactions with customers are available, up-to-date and in good order.

❑ Actively seek opportunities for improving working relationships with customers.

❑ Use own behaviour to convey consistently a positive image of the organisation to current and potential customers, and to colleagues.

❑ Work to support other colleagues in presenting a positive image of the organisation to current and potential customers.

27 | Recognise and exploit opportunities for up-selling and cross-selling

❑ Assess information provided by customers about their buying needs and interests for the potential for up-selling or cross-selling.

❑ Question customers about their need for, or interest in, other products and services.

❑ Provide customers with relevant information about other products and services which may interest them.

❑ Inform relevant colleagues about further sales opportunities which can be pursued with the customer.

❑ Remain sensitive to the needs of the customer when pursuing opportunities for up-selling and cross-selling.

❑ Record information about the customer's buying needs and interests in order for future opportunities for up-selling or cross-selling.

Generate customer interest in products and services

❏ Structure and control communication with customers, while maintaining flexibility, to achieve the defined sales objectives.

❏ Convey clearly, accurately, and at a level and pace to promote understanding, the advantages to the customer of the product or service.

❏ Establish and reinforce during contact the customer's needs and interests, in relation to the product or service.

❏ Present information relating to the product or service in such a manner as to generate and maintain customer interest.

❏ Correctly interpret and act upon buying signals given by the customer.

❏ Give the customer every opportunity to discuss the purchase fully, and examine products or services.

❏ Suggest an alternative course of action where the product does not interest the customer.

❏ Ensure that procedures are carried out in order to generate customer interest and that these conform with organisational and legal requirements, where appropriate.

❏ Assess your personal performance in generating customer interest and take steps to improve performance in any areas of weakness.

29 | Plan and prepare for sales negotiations

❑ Ensure that the role(s) and level(s) of responsibility of the customer's representative(s) are accurately established prior to negotiations.

❑ Identify and confirm the customer's main requirements from the negotiations.

❑ Clearly identify and prioritise the objectives of the negotiations.

❑ Where possible, research and assess the strength of the customer's negotiating stance prior to negotiations taking place.

❑ Identify and agree what flexibility is to be allowed over the price, specifications and other key aspects of the good or service to be sold.

❑ Obtain authorisation for any additional concessions.

❑ Identify and formulate solutions to potential problems in negotiations.

❑ Ensure that resources for the sales negotiations are identified and are available in a serviceable and safe condition.

❑ Make sure that all people involved in the negotiations are fully briefed and prepared in advance.

❑ Check that advance proposals to the customer fall within organisational, legal and regulatory requirements.

Agree with potential customers the nature and time of follow up calls from others

❑ Ensure that the potential customer's genuine interest in products and services is confirmed.

❑ Agree and confirm with the customer the most suitable follow up activity.

❑ Confirm with the customer the most suitable time for follow up activity.

❑ Provide relevant people with accurate details of follow up activity to permit follow up activity to take place.

❑ Provide supporting information to aid sales activity to relevant people where necessary.

Getting to yes

This section is about the forms of support that you should offer to customers.

The checklists will help you to

■ solve problems or objections the customer has

■ prepare proposals that will gain agreement to the terms of sale.

31 | Generate solutions to customer problems and objections

❑ Establish and clarify accurately and clearly, through tactful questioning and sympathetic discussion, any customer objections to products or services.

❑ Convey relevant information and proposals to meet any objections promptly and accurately to the customer.

❑ Formulate and agree solutions to any problems that satisfy customer needs and objections by the customer where possible.

❑ Where customer objections cannot be resolved or where legal or regulatory frameworks prevent responses to objections, propose an alternative course of action to overcome the problem or objection.

❑ Enure that records of customer objections which cannot be resolved are clear, and that they accurately specify the reasons for the inability to resolve the objection.

Formulate and make proposals to agree the terms of sale

32

- ❑ Formulate and present proposals that meet the customer's requirements and organisational sales objectives.

- ❑ Ensure that proposals correspond to prioritised objectives and are within parameters set for key variables.

- ❑ Seek and confirm authorisation for any concessions, e.g. variations in the terms of trade.

- ❑ Seek to anticipate any problems arising from the customer's requirements, formulate solutions and have them available prior to the presentation of proposals to the customer.

- ❑ Identify and highlight those elements of the proposals that meet the customer's requirements.

- ❑ Make sure that where the customer's main requirements have changed, new proposals are made to meet them within the organisation's sales objectives.

- ❑ Ensure that proposals to the customer fall within organisational, legal and regulatory requirements.

- ❑ Present proposals to customers in a format which facilitates understanding and details all necessary terms of sale.

Conclude the sale

This section is about how to complete the sales process and close the sale.

The checklists will help you to

■ negotiate the terms of sale to arrive at a mutually satisfactory contract.

33 | Conclude agreements on contracts

❑ Identify and address unresolved elements of the sales proposals and present proposals for their resolution to satisfy customer needs and account objectives where possible.

❑ Ensure that contract proposals to the customer fall within organisational, legal and regulatory requirements.

❑ Prepare final contract proposals to meet the customer's outstanding requirements, and ensure that these proposals conform to parameters set for key variables and sales objectives.

❑ Conclude agreement on contracts for the supply of the product or service to the mutual satisfaction of both parties.

❑ Accurately summarise and record the agreement with the customer in written form.

❑ Check that any contracts with the customer conform with organisational, legal and regulatory requirements, and consult company or external experts if necessary.

❑ Keep in a secure and accessible location formal records of the contract, making certain that this documentation conforms to organisational, legal and regulatory requirements.

Agree terms and conditions and close sale   34

- ❏ Confirm by effective questioning and discussion the customer's willingness to commit themselves to a purchase.

- ❏ Identify items requiring agreement or further discussion and resolve these issues to the satisfaction of both parties.

- ❏ Reach agreement on the supply of products and services that meet both parties' requirements.

- ❏ Agree the terms of sale with the customer and confirm the customer's satisfaction with their order.

- ❏ Note the reasons why the customer's expectation cannot be met and why a sale cannot progress, and supply the analysis to appropriate people where required.

- ❏ Formalise and fully document any agreement with the customer according to organisational and legal requirements.

- ❏ Submit formal quotations where required.

- ❏ Strictly adhere to any legal or regulatory frameworks which affect the final terms of sale and ensure compliance with the limits of those frameworks.

CHAPTER 4

Tenders, key accounts and major projects

Evaluate the offer to tender

This section is about completing the necessary preparatory work when evaluating offers to tender.

The checklist will help you to

■ make evaluations of documentation concerning the tender.

35 | Evaluate tender enquiry documentation

❑ Confirm details in the tender documents, and check and clarify any queries with the issuing organisation.

❑ Accurately summarise the main points of the tender document and pass information on to other staff for their comments.

❑ Ensure that any points in tender documents that may cause concern are clarified with people who are able to provide advice and guidance on relevant issues.

❑ Ensure that contact with customers is strictly in line with the conditions specified in the invitation to tender.

❑ Clearly establish the status and financial viability of the organisation issuing the tender.

❑ Initiate further investigations, where necessary, before decisions on invitations to tender are made.

❑ Evaluate the tender against agreed criteria and discuss the analysis with appropriate people.

❑ Ensure that recommendations on whether to proceed are provided clearly and accurately to relevant people.

Replying to the tender

This section is about helping you to reply to the tender offer.

The checklists will help you to

■ evaluate what will be required to fulfil a tender and what this will cost

■ make recommendations concerning the preparation of the tender.

36 Assess the resource requirements and costs of a tender

❏ Assess and establish the resources needed to meet the requirements of the tender and that their availability is confirmed.

❏ Identify potential problems in securing resources, and ensure that any potential for costs to increase is identified.

❏ Estimate the cost of individual items, with potential variations in cost identified, and a summary of total costs calculated.

❏ Prepare a draft schedule of deliveries and payments, which takes into account both the customer's delivery needs and own organisation's delivery capacity and cash-flow requirements.

❏ Present costings and resource implications in a written format to relevant stakeholders.

Submit a tender application   37

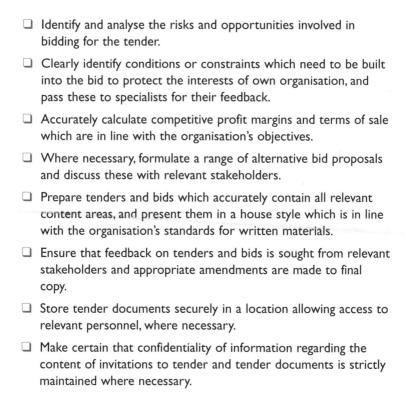

❑ Identify and analyse the risks and opportunities involved in bidding for the tender.

❑ Clearly identify conditions or constraints which need to be built into the bid to protect the interests of own organisation, and pass these to specialists for their feedback.

❑ Accurately calculate competitive profit margins and terms of sale which are in line with the organisation's objectives.

❑ Where necessary, formulate a range of alternative bid proposals and discuss these with relevant stakeholders.

❑ Prepare tenders and bids which accurately contain all relevant content areas, and present them in a house style which is in line with the organisation's standards for written materials.

❑ Ensure that feedback on tenders and bids is sought from relevant stakeholders and appropriate amendments are made to final copy.

❑ Store tender documents securely in a location allowing access to relevant personnel, where necessary.

❑ Make certain that confidentiality of information regarding the content of invitations to tender and tender documents is strictly maintained where necessary.

Presenting to key accounts

This section is about how to give a presentation to one of your key account customers.

The checklists will help you to

■ prepare for the presentation

■ present information to the key account customer

■ promote the organisation's products and services

■ make an assessment of the success of the presentation.

38 Present information and arguments on the benefits of using the organisation for the supply of products and services

❏ Secure and confirm the presence and role of all of the presentation team members, explain their roles clearly to the customer and invite the team members to introduce themselves.

❏ Present clearly and accurately to the customer information about the organisation and relevant products and services.

❏ Deliver the presentation in a manner and at a pace suitable for the audience.

❏ Encourage the customers to ask questions and confirm their understanding of the main points.

❏ Turn signals given by the customer into opportunities to illustrate how products and services would be of benefit to them.

❏ Counter the customer's objections and queries with clear and positive responses.

❏ Ensure that terms and conditions for products and services are explained clearly, and that opportunities to negotiate are taken where it is within the job holder's authority.

❏ Where possible, take opportunities during or after the presentation to gain a commitment to, or progress, sales.

❏ Leave relevant contact details, promotional literature and samples with the customers and agree follow up arrangements with them.

Develop and agree the format, content and approach of major sales presentations with team members

❑ Identify the relevant content and objectives for a presentation aimed at meeting the identified buying needs and interests of the customer.

❑ Agree the methods and style of the presentation which are considered relevant for the particular audience.

❑ Confirm the roles which different team members are to fulfil.

❑ Prepare and rehearse the structure and sequence of the presentation.

❑ Manage resources so that all team members are adequately prepared in order to fulfil their agreed role.

❑ Check that resources which are required for the presentation are in place and ready to use.

❑ Check equipment.

❑ Review support materials and confirm that these are prepared to the required standard and are available in the correct quantities.

❑ Devise a strategy to overcome objections presented by the customer and agree strategy with relevant people.

❑ Agree a time and place for the presentation with the customer.

40 Prepare for and present information to promote the organisation's products and services to key account customers

❑ Identify and confirm the customer's needs and interests in relation to the product or service.

❑ Establish the duration, nature of, and audience for, presentations to ensure the most suitable format and presentation methods.

❑ Formulate, determine and prepare the objectives and content of the presentation, and the media for the presentation.

❑ Make certain equipment is secured and is in a safe and operable condition, and test before use.

❑ Ensure that proposals and support materials are produced to the required standard and are available in the correct quantities where necessary.

❑ Present information clearly, accurately and at a pace that aids understanding.

❑ Ensure that the information presented to the customer conforms to the duration, structure and content of the planned presentation.

❑ During and after the presentation answer customers' questions sympathetically and satisfactorily, and promptly provide additional information where necessary.

❑ Use divergences from the prepared plan to maintain the sales objectives.

❑ Complete evaluations of presentations, checking them for their ability to meet set objectives and use conclusions to inform future practice or development of own performance.

Prepare for a sales presentation 41

❑ Clarify the customer's objectives and particular needs and interests in products and services are clarified, where required.

❑ Plan the presentation to meet the client's goals and progress the sale.

❑ Clearly identify the variables which apply to the presentation and use these variables to inform the preparation of the presentation.

❑ Identify and check all resources, especially the technical ones, for the presentation, and confirm their availability and reliability.

❑ Secure alternative resources where necessary and plan back-ups and contingencies.

❑ Ensure that the presentation contains all necessary information and ideas.

❑ Structure the presentation in order to maximise the impact of the information and ideas contained within it.

❑ Where relevant, supply proposals to accompany the sales presentation to the customer within adequate timescales.

❑ Anticipate and plan for potential divergences from the sales presentation, prepare alternative ideas and courses of action.

42 | Give and evaluate a sales presentation

❏ Present information clearly and in a style and manner which is appropriate to the audience, ensures their safety and inspires their confidence.

❏ Ensure that the length, structure and substance of the presentation conform with the pre-prepared plan.

❏ Use appropriate resources and presentation aids to enhance the presentation.

❏ Welcome and address customers' questions and comments both during and after the presentation.

❏ Promptly and accurately supply additional information required by the customer.

❏ Attempt, where possible, to take opportunities during or after the presentation to gain a commitment to, or progress, sales.

❏ Evaluate the presentation against objectives, and use the conclusions to improve the preparation and delivery of future presentations.

Co-ordinating the project team

This section is about the types of organisation that are required when running a major project.

The checklists will help you to

■ make clear what the project is to cover in terms of its scope and definition

■ create plans that will help attain the goals of the project

■ organise the running of activities, resources and plans

■ make sure that all relevant people are kept informed

■ give the project team the support it requires

■ bring project activities to a close

■ make contributions to evaluating the project's planning and its implementation.

43 | Contribute to project preparation

❏ Assist in the selection of team members who are able to make an effective contribution to the project's objectives.

❏ Recommend roles for the project team, and allocate tasks in a way which is realistic and equitable.

❏ Outline clear lines of responsibility and accountability which take account of team members' other responsibilities.

❏ Propose meeting schedules, reporting, control and communication methods which are consistent with the project plans.

❏ Contribute to effective opportunities for team development.

❏ Research and recommend feasible and cost-effective methods of obtaining the necessary physical resources.

❏ Study and advise on efficient and effective methods of managing the necessary physical resources and finances which are consistent with organisational requirements.

❏ Check all aspects of the project's resourcing and control methods with relevant people, and take account of their feedback when making revisions.

Clarify the project's scope and definition 44

❑ Identify with relevant people the project's scope and definition to the level of detail needed for effective planning.

❑ Review the links between the project's scope and definition and the wider organisational objectives.

❑ Identify key stakeholders' interests in the project.

❑ Study and spell out the main contingencies which may occur during the running of the project.

❑ Outline the main risks associated with the project.

❑ Provide realistic and informed views on the feasibility of the project's scope and definition to relevant people.

❑ Clearly establish your own level of responsibility and accountability for project activities, resources and decisions.

❑ Clearly confirm your understanding of the project's scope and definition with relevant people inside and outside the organisation, and with partners, and take account of their feedback.

45 | Provide plans to achieve the project's goals

❏ Ensure that plans for the project are consistent with the agreed scope and definition and known constraints.

❏ Break down the project work into tasks which are manageable, measurable, and achievable.

❏ Specify links, dependencies, schedules, evaluation methods and hand over procedures which are appropriate to the project and its work.

❏ Propose effective measures to deal with identified contingencies and risks.

❏ Realistically estimate and cost the human and physical resources required to carry out the project's tasks.

❏ Base your plans on previous experience and the good practice of relevant people.

❏ Check all aspects of the project plans with the relevant people and take account of their feedback when you make revisions.

Co-ordinate activities, resources and plans 46

❏ Monitor and evaluate project work in a way which is consistent with the agreed plans.

❏ Accurately measure progress against plans and identify emerging risks and difficulties and their causes.

❏ Obtain clear authorisation for all stages of work to start, continue or finish.

❏ Clearly inform the higher-level manager of any emerging problems or risks in good time for remedial action to be taken.

❏ Keep activities and resources in line with the project's plans or seek approval for any amendments to plans and resources from the higher-level manager.

❏ Recommend changes in project activities, plans and resources in a way which keeps disruption to a minimum.

❏ Make any adjustments to activities, resources and plans with the knowledge and agreement of the team and accurately record and store these adjustments.

❏ Inform the higher-level manager promptly and clearly of any need to review the project's scope and definition with the sponsor.

47 | Keep stakeholders informed of project progress

❑ Provide the key stakeholders with timely, forward-looking and relevant information which is consistent with the project plans and helpful to the project achieving its goals.

❑ Supply team members and higher-level managers with effective opportunities to contribute to the information you provide.

❑ Ensure that the content of the information meets your stakeholders' needs, while maintaining agreements on confidentiality.

❑ Distribute information in styles and formats most appropriate to the types of stakeholders involved.

❑ Build and maintain distribution methods that are effective in reaching the key stakeholders.

❑ Actively seek and assess information from stakeholders that may affect the running of the project.

Support the project team   48

☐ Consistently motivate team members to fulfil the tasks allocated to them with commitment and enthusiasm.

☐ Systematically provide team members with clear, accurate and up-to-date information appropriate to the role which they play in the project.

☐ Provide regular opportunities for team members to undertake activities which will contribute to their own development and that of the project.

☐ Actively seek information from team members on project progress and their views on the project's effectiveness.

☐ Correctly and promptly identify problems which team members are experiencing.

☐ Provide team members with the support and encouragement they need to achieve their objectives throughout the lifetime of the project.

49 Complete project activities

❑ Confirm that all the project's goals have been achieved to the agreed schedule, costs and quality criteria.

❑ Hand over all deliverables according to agreed procedures.

❑ Resolve any hand over problems to the sponsor's satisfaction or seek the support of relevant people

❑ Clearly inform the higher-level manager that the agreed project outcomes have been achieved and seek their approval to close the project.

❑ Collect information from relevant people on the effectiveness of the project and their level of satisfaction with it.

❑ Confirm the completion of the project with the team and promptly bring all associated work to an end in a way that is consistent with your project plans.

❑ Complete all the necessary procedures relating to finance, resources and personnel in accordance with organisational requirements.

❑ Ensure that all records and documents relating to the project are accurate, complete and securely stored for future use.

Contribute to the evaluation of project planning and implementation | 50

❑ Collect, check and collate information relating to the planning and implementation of the project, in a way that will assist effective evaluation.

❑ Include information that covers the perspectives of all key stakeholders.

❑ Assist relevant people to compare what was planned, what actually happened, and what changes had to be made to plans, project definition and scope.

❑ Propose feasible causes for variations to plans and the key lessons to be drawn from the project.

❑ Record and store your evaluation in a way that can be used to inform future projects.

CHAPTER 5

Presenting the product or service

 **Demonstration**

This section is about how to demonstrate your organisation's products and services to your customers.

The checklists will help you to

■ make the correct preparations for a demonstration

■ carry out the demonstration to customers

■ meet the customers requirements for goods.

51 | Prepare for a demonstration of products and services

❑ Clearly establish the customer's needs and interests, in relation to products and services.

❑ Agree with the customer the length of, nature of, and audience for the demonstration.

❑ Clearly agree and deliver the objectives of the sales demonstration, in order to drive its preparation and delivery.

❑ Identify, make available and, where necessary, prepare for use any resources needed for the demonstration.

❑ Prepare and organise the structure of the demonstration in order to provide all necessary information and promote the features and benefits of the product and service.

❑ Ensure that, where relevant, proposals accompanying the sales demonstration are made before meeting the customer.

❑ Recognise, and prepare for, possible problems or constraints on the demonstration.

❑ Anticipate, and take appropriate courses of action for, potential customer responses to the demonstration.

Demonstrate the features and benefits of products and services to customers

52

❏ Ensure that the resources needed for the demonstration are at hand, ready for use and in good condition.

❏ Check own understanding and competence in relation to the product or service in preparation for the demonstration, and get additional support, further training or advice if necessary.

❏ Undertake demonstrations in a style and manner that is appropriate for the audience and ensures individual's safety.

❏ Supply the audience with clear information about the objectives, content and method of the demonstration.

❏ Confirm that all members of the audience are able to observe and engage in the demonstration.

❏ Explain during the demonstration the advantages and benefits of the product or service.

❏ Where appropriate and safe, invite members of the audience to use the product or service once it has been demonstrated.

❏ Invite the audience to ask questions and seek clarification.

❏ Where possible, take opportunities to progress sales at the time of the demonstration.

53 Confirm the availability of goods to meet customers' requirements

❑ Check that customers' requirements are identified accurately from information provided by the customers.

❑ Identify items which meet customers' requirements for type, quantity and quality of goods.

❑ Confirm the source and availability of items to meet customers' requirements.

❑ Ensure that information about items is accurate and is given to customers promptly.

❑ Make prompt arrangements to obtain items not immediately available, and keep the customer informed clearly of the action taken.

Order processing and delivery

This section is about processing the customer's order and ensuring the hand over is completed.

The checklists will help you to

■ follow the necessary procedures when recording and processing an order

■ make the preparations for handing the goods over to the customer.

54 | Record and process customers' orders

❑ Confirm the identity and credit status of customers accurately, by reference to authorised sources of information.

❑ Check for accuracy records of customers' requirements.

❑ Ensure that information about customers' requirements is passed promptly to those responsible for filling orders.

❑ Record accurately information required to support sales and make the information available promptly to those issuing invoices.

❑ When the order cannot be processed, note the reasons accurately and report them promptly to an authorised person.

❑ Check that customers are informed promptly and politely when their order cannot be fulfilled within normal timescales.

❑ Store information securely and make certain that it is available only to those who have a right to it.

Prepare for the hand over of goods to the customer

55

❑ Prepare and hand over goods to the customer in accordance with sales agreements.

❑ Confirm that, where required, arrangements for the transfer of ownership are in place.

❑ Check that any and all modifications and other requirements are carried out in line with agreements made with the customer.

❑ Complete accurately records of hand over preparations.

❑ Ensure that all documentation required for the hand over of goods is complete and accurate.

After sales support and service

This section is about offering the customer support and further services after the sale has been completed.

The checklists will help you to

■ check on the delivery of the goods and ensure any required installation has been completed

■ ensure that customers are satisfied with their purchase and the level of service they have received

■ make sure that the customer knows how to use the products or services properly

■ give assistance to customers during their initial use of the products or services

■ make arrangements for maintaining and/or servicing the products or services

■ solve problems customers have with the products or services

■ collect information from customers and use this information to improve on the current service delivery or create new delivery systems

■ create solutions to problems that seem to be common to all customers.

56 | Monitor the delivery and implementation of products and services

❏ Confirm the punctual delivery of all components of products and services.

❏ Ensure that where components of products and services cannot be delivered according to schedule, a mutually acceptable agreement is reached about delivery dates of the unavailable components.

❏ Confirm the organisation's commitment to service and delivery.

❏ Assess the impact of any late deliveries on customers.

❏ Take all steps to minimise the negative effects of any delays or service failures on customers.

❏ Offer all assistance, within the limits of own authority and capability, to provide technical advice and assistance during the implementation of products and services.

❏ Agree with customers the nature and level of assistance required during the implementation of products and services.

❏ Where required, make arrangements with appropriate colleagues to provide any assistance to customers.

❏ Resolve, where possible, the customer's queries and problems during the implementation of products and services.

❏ Help customers overcome problems outside own immediate area of competence by seeking additional support.

Confirm with customers their satisfaction with products and services

❑ Use customer surveys or other feedback mechanisms to assess the customer's satisfaction with products and services.

❑ Contact customers on delivery, and at agreed intervals where appropriate, to confirm their satisfaction with products and services.

❑ Obtain feedback about the customer's satisfaction with products and services from all relevant parties.

❑ Gather information on, investigate and make proposals for resolving any areas of dissatisfaction expressed by the customer.

❑ Make offers to customers to help resolve areas of dissatisfaction within limits of own authority.

❑ Seek help from appropriate authorities to resolve areas of dissatisfaction outside limits of own authority.

❑ Obtain feedback about customers' satisfaction and pass on information to relevant people in order to inform the development of future practice and, where relevant, product and service design.

58 Demonstrate to customers how to use products and services effectively

❑ Agree a convenient place and time for the demonstration with the customer.

❑ Make sure that products and services and other resources are available at the times agreed with the customer, and are booked out for demonstrations.

❑ Set up demonstrations in a manner which protects the products and services, equipment and the people who are present.

❑ Conduct demonstrations in a way that ensures that all those present can see what is happening.

❑ Explain the purpose of the demonstration and the features and benefits of the products and services being demonstrated to those present.

❑ Where regulations and safety permit, give people who will be using the products and services an opportunity to try them out themselves.

❑ Respond positively to, and counter constructively with further information and persuasive arguments, comments and queries from people attending the demonstration.

Support customers during their initial use of products and services

❑ Agree a plan of support with the customer and carry this out to the customer's satisfaction.

❑ Contact customers on delivery and at agreed intervals to check on their progress in using the products and services.

❑ Resolve customers' queries effectively or refer them to other forms of support if the job holder is unable to help.

❑ Make suggestions to the customer to help them use and get the best from products and services more effectively.

❑ Access other forms of support where required.

60 | Arrange for the servicing and maintenance of products and services

❏ Agree with the customer the service and maintenance arrangements for products and services.

❏ Recommend to customers appropriate contracts for service, maintenance, repair and insurance.

❏ Ensure that customers' requests for maintenance and services are authorised in line with agreements made with them.

❏ Agree a price for providing a service or maintenance with customers in instances where no prior agreement is made.

❏ Make arrangements to provide a service or maintenance to products and services as agreed with the customer.

❏ Pass on details about maintenance and repair to the people who will do it.

❏ Confirm the customer's satisfaction with the service or maintenance services provided.

Co-ordinate solutions to problems with products and services

❑ Agree the nature of any problems with products and services with the customer.

❑ Follow up any problems with products and services and identify reasons for the difficulties.

❑ Make agreements with the customer to satisfy their needs for the repair, maintenance or replacement of products and services.

❑ Make agreements with maintenance and service providers to enable service to be provided to the customer.

❑ Supply people who provide maintenance and repair services with all essential information to enable the service or repair to take place.

❑ Re-organise arrangements for repair and maintenance in instances where the customer, or those completing the service or repair, are unable to keep the agreed appointment.

❑ Confirm the customer's satisfaction with repair and maintenance services.

62 Obtain and use feedback from customer

❏ Ensure that comments on organisational services are consistently sought from customers.

❏ Monitor and evaluate all complaints from customers about products/services.

❏ Use all opportunities, including criticisms and compliments, to monitor and evaluate relevant products/services.

❏ Seek new opportunities to gain customer feedback.

❏ Use existing feedback mechanisms to gather information and record outcomes thoroughly.

❏ Store customer feedback in the most appropriate place.

Marshal customer feedback from internal and external systems

63

❑ Monitor, evaluate and improve current methods of obtaining customer feedback where necessary.

❑ Examine, on a routine and regular basis, information relating to customer feedback for relevance to own area of responsibility.

❑ Actively seek feedback on service systems from customers.

❑ Using customer feedback, identify and communicate necessary service improvements in own area of responsibility.

❑ Communicate conclusions for necessary service improvements to appropriate individuals.

64   Modify current service systems in response to customer feedback

❏ Propose modifications to others based on an analysis of current systems and customer feedback.

❏ Systematically improve procedures within own area of responsibility, based on customer feedback.

❏ Ensure that, where appropriate, current service systems are modified by colleagues as a result of own influence and customer feedback.

❏ Modify current service systems in response to continuing feedback from own colleagues.

❏ Communicate implications of modifications to service systems to the appropriate colleague(s).

Identify and interpret problems affecting customers

❑ Ensure that, where necessary, customers are questioned thoroughly and sensitively to gather all relevant data about their perceived problems with product or service.

❑ Accurately identify and acknowledge customers' perceptions of problems.

❑ Gather and systematically analyse and prioritise all potential information relevant to the customer's problem.

❑ Using own perceptions and information gained from customers, clearly summarise any problems that customers may have, and the solutions they seek or which are desirable.

❑ Design responses to protect customers from unnecessary worry.

❑ Ensure that, where necessary, information about problems affecting customers is passed to the relevant people.

66 Take action to deliver solutions

❑ Take action promptly to solve customers' problems.

❑ Provide to the appropriate people clear information about recurring problems or complaints and effective solutions to them.

❑ Ensure that delivery is monitored and suitably modified to resolve any problems.

❑ Present alternative solutions to the customer.

❑ Give accurate advice to customers on relevant alternative sources of assistance.

❑ Follow organisational procedures at all times.

❑ Supply feedback to relevant people to influence the improvement of procedures for customer service.

Innovate and monitor new service delivery systems

❑ Continually monitor and review service systems in own area of responsibility.

❑ Introduce innovations that respond to customer requirements.

❑ Base innovations on a thorough analysis of appropriate data and predictions of future customer needs.

❑ Implement innovations in collaboration with colleagues in response to customer feedback and through own influence.

❑ Monitor and adjust changes in service delivery where necessary.

❑ Initiate any necessary changes in collaboration with others.

68 | Solve generic customer problems

❑ Gather and systematically analyse information relevant to persistent customer problems.

❑ Seek advice from all relevant sources for solutions to customer problems.

❑ Identify alternative solutions for the customer.

❑ Ensure that solutions for mutual gain are cost-effective for both parties.

❑ Thoroughly explore flexibility in organisational service systems to solve generic customer problems.

❑ Make persistent attempts to solve generic customer problems within own limits of authority.

❑ Inform customers of action taken to solve generic service problems.

CHAPTER 6

Pricing

Proposed price

This section is about making proposals to customers on the price of products and services in order to agree a sale.

The checklists will help you to

■ create proposals on the terms of sale that meet the requirements of your organisation and the customer

■ calculate the price of purchases

■ carry out negotiations with the customer about the terms of sales and reach an agreement.

69 Formulate and make proposals to agree the terms of sale

❑ Check that proposals are formulated and made which both meet the customer's requirements and promote the achievement of organisational sales objectives.

❑ Make sure that proposals to customers correspond to prioritised objectives, and are within parameters set for key variables.

❑ Seek, where necessary, authorisation for concessions that fall outside the parameters set for key variables, and confirm these concessions with the appropriate authority.

❑ Anticipate and formulate solutions to potential problems arising from the mismatch of proposals and the customer's requirements.

❑ Accurately identify, and highlight to the customer, specific features of proposals which meet customer's requirements.

❑ Amend or make new proposals to satisfy the changes where customers' main requirements have changed.

❑ Ensure that proposals to the customer fall within organisational, legal and regulatory requirements.

❑ Conduct negotiations in a manner which helps the customer's understanding of the proposals, creates goodwill and promotes a positive image of self and the organisation.

❑ Seek clarification of the customer's understanding, and respond to their queries and objections, in a manner that is satisfactory to the client and the company.

Calculate the price of customers' purchases   70

❑ Identify accurately and exactly the price of items.

❑ Resolve problems in pricing goods promptly by using available sources of information and advice.

❑ Check that all calculations are correct.

❑ Conduct pricing calculations at a pace which balances the need for accuracy and customer care with the need to process sales quickly.

❑ Inspect purchases visually for condition and quality as they are processed.

❑ When faults or discrepancies in items are observed, take action promptly to provide customers with satisfactory products.

❑ Conduct all transactions courteously and in a manner appropriate to the customer and the context.

71 Negotiate and agree the terms of sale

- ❏ Identify and discuss with the customer any objections to the sales proposals.

- ❏ Conduct all contacts with customers in a manner aimed at enhancing goodwill and promoting the working relationship with them.

- ❏ Make proposals to resolve aspects of the proposal for which agreement has not been reached.

- ❏ Confirm that final proposals to customers correspond to prioritised objectives and are within parameters set for key variables.

- ❏ Finalise agreement on the supply of the product or service to the mutual satisfaction of both parties where possible.

- ❏ Accurately summarise and record agreement(s) with the customer.

- ❏ Ensure that all agreements with the customer conform to organisational, legal and regulatory requirements.

- ❏ Keep formal records of the agreement within organisational, legal and regulatory requirements.

- ❏ Supply accurate details of the outcomes of negotiations to appropriate people within own organisation.

Financing

This section is about organising financial arrangements for the customer for the sale of products and services.

The checklists will help you to

■ identify what your customers' needs are regarding financial arrangements

■ organise the financial arrangements required by the customer

■ process the customer's application for finance services

■ prepare and present to the customer proposals and quotations for the supply of products and services

■ process the payments from sales.

72 | Identify the customer's finance needs

❑ Accurately calculate the exact payment balance for goods owed by the customer.

❑ Ensure that the amount of potential borrowing required by the customer is accurately calculated.

❑ Agree any borrowing requirements with the customer and identify their preferred finance options.

❑ Accurately identify the types of finance options which can be offered to the customer.

❑ Accurately complete all necessary documentation.

❑ Ensure that legal and regulatory requirements are strictly adhered to at all times.

Agree finance arrangements with the customer to enable them to buy products or services — 73

❑ Ensure that the customer is informed about the terms and conditions which apply to specific finance options.

❑ Fully discuss the customer's concerns, and supply any necessary additional information to help the customer select the most suitable finance option.

❑ Accurately supply, where necessary, written proposals for finance arrangements to the customer in the required format.

❑ Agree the finance arrangements which best fit the customer's requirements.

❑ Take opportunities to promote sales of additional financial services where appropriate and within strict legal and organisational rules.

❑ Present revised proposals to customers where appropriate.

❑ Refer to an appropriate authority, where necessary, issues which arise during the arrangement of finance that are outside of own remit.

❑ Accurately complete all necessary documentation.

❑ Ensure that legal and regulatory requirements are strictly adhered to at all times.

74 | Process finance applications

❑ Gather all necessary information to enable applications for finance to proceed.

❑ Complete all necessary credit checks satisfactorily.

❑ Obtain, where necessary, further information from the customer where checks reveal inconsistencies or discrepancies in details supplied by the customer.

❑ Seek advice and assistance from an appropriate authority where problems occur with finance applications.

❑ Inform the customer clearly and accurately of decisions about arrangements for the drawdown of facilities and the terms and conditions that apply to the facility.

❑ Take action to process the drawdown of financial facilities.

❑ Accurately complete all necessary documentation.

❑ Ensure that legal and regulatory requirements, including confidentiality of information, are stricly adhered to at all times.

Prepare proposals and quotations for the supply of products and services — 75

❏ Make certain that the customer's requirements are understood, and that matters requiring clarification are resolved.

❏ Identify and build into the quotation any conditions or constraints that will protect the interests of own organisation.

❏ Check that the profit margin and proposed terms of sale stated in the quotation are in line with the objectives of own organisation.

❏ Ensure that quotations supplied to customers are competitive, provide the required level of detail, and are supplied within stipulated timescales.

❏ Calculate and write into the quotation any discounts or special offers.

❏ Where required, prepare proposals and quotations in the house style and in line with the presentation requirements of the customer.

❏ Protect any confidential information and consult appropriate people prior to dispatch to the customer.

❏ Secure proposals and quotations in a location that allows access to authorised people.

76	**Present proposals and quotations for the supply of products and services**

❑ Agree with the customer the nature and format of information contained in proposals.

❑ Present the proposal clearly in a manner which helps the customer understand its contents, and which promotes the organisation and its products and services.

❑ Provide customers with opportunities to ask questions and seek clarification on all aspects of the proposal.

❑ Identify, discuss and recognise customers' objections and, where appropriate, counter these through logical argument and explanation.

❑ Maintain the limits of personal authority during post-proposal negotiations with the customer.

❑ Where negotiations are beyond the limits of personal authority, seek authority from appropriate people or refer negotiations to them.

❑ Encourage and enable customers to commit themselves to a purchase.

❑ Confirm with the customer the order and terms of sale.

Process sales payments 77

- ❏ Inform customers of the amount(s) due clearly and accurately.
- ❏ Confirm the amount given and any change required.
- ❏ Confirm authorisation for accepting non-cash payments, especially when the value of the item exceeds specified limits.
- ❏ Inform the customer tactfully when authorisation cannot be obtained for non-cash payments.
- ❏ Complete accurately all documentation associated with payments.
- ❏ Identify and remedy promptly any discrepancies and errors.
- ❏ Store payments securely and protect them from theft.
- ❏ Offer assistance in packaging and transporting purchases, when these faculties are available.
- ❏ Ensure that the transaction is conducted courteously and in a manner appropriate to the customer and the context.

Part exchange

This section is about evaluating the acceptability of goods offered in part exchange for products and services.

The checklists will help you to

■ check on the ownership and status of goods offered

■ make an assessment about the condition of the goods.

78 Identify the status and ownership of any goods offered in part exchange

❏ Verify the customer's ownership of goods for part exchange.

❏ Identify the interest of third parties and note any restrictions affecting the transfer of ownership.

❏ Verify the accuracy of recorded usage, where possible.

❏ Where relevant, establish and confirm the date of manufacture and registration.

❏ Identify the make, model and any additions or modifications to standard specifications.

❏ Authenticate the documentation relating to the goods.

❏ Discuss any discrepancies with the customer, or refer them to an appropriate authority where action is outside of own remit of authority.

❏ Pass any suspicions about the ownership of goods to an appropriate authority without delay.

Assess the condition of goods for part exchange | 79

- ❏ Evaluate and assess the serviceability of goods and their future usability.

- ❏ Assess the condition of cosmetic features of the goods.

- ❏ Analyse, check for accuracy, and record service records and other relevant documentation.

- ❏ Accurately identify and note sales refurbishment work.

- ❏ Accurately record in the required format the assessment of goods for part exchange.

- ❏ Ensure that appraisals of goods for part exchange are stored correctly or passed to the appropriate authority where necessary.

CHAPTER 7

Contributing to the marketing effort

The marketing effort

This section is about looking at the marketing of products and services and ways in which it can be used to increase sales.

The checklists will help you to

- make informed contributions on how to market the organisation's goods and services

- ensure that any identified patterns and trends in customer services are communicated across the organisation

- make contributions to evaluations concerned with changes to customer service and assist with those changes that will lead to improvements in the service.

80 | Make recommendations on the marketing of products and services

❑ Gather information on, evaluate, and draw conclusions about market conditions.

❑ Make recommendations based on the evaluation of market conditions and the current or potential value and competitiveness of the organisation's products and services.

❑ Consult colleagues at regular intervals about the image and perceived value and competitiveness of the organisation's products and services.

❑ Provide recommendations to relevant people on the marketing of the organisation's products and services.

❑ Provide feedback to relevant people on marketing methods and policies currently in use.

❑ Ensure that information that supports marketing recommendations is valid, reliable and timely.

❑ Provide recommendations in the required organisational format.

Communicate patterns and trends in customer service within the organisation | 81

❑ Ensure that measures of customer service are clearly presented in the appropriate form and are based on accurate information.

❑ Evaluate present customer service against current patterns and trends provided by the organisation.

❑ Make predictions about customer requirements based on the accurate interpretation of patterns and trends.

❑ Provide concise information, which accurately illustrates patterns and trends, to appropriately targeted individuals.

❑ Check that evaluation takes full account of existing organisational criteria for customer service.

82	**Contribute to the evaluation of changes and help initiate those designed to improve service to customers**

❏ Ensure that outcomes of changes to improve customer service are systematically monitored using all available feedback.

❏ Identify the implications of changes to products/services and communicate these to the appropriate colleagues.

❏ Present recommendations on the effectiveness of changes designed to improve customer service to the appropriate colleague(s).

❏ Take action, within own area of authority, to remedy shortfalls in customer service.

❏ Alert others to changes needed to improve customer service.

❏ Introduce initiatives that respond to customer requirements and are within own area of authority.

❏ Ensure that any actions and initiatives are based on a thorough analysis of appropriate data, and take account of any predicted future customer needs.

❏ Clearly present proposed changes outside own area of authority.

 **Innovation**

This section is about identifying ways of improving existing products and services and introducing completely new ones.

The checklists will help you to

■ agree on plans that will introduce customers to any new or improved products and services

■ agree on who will have responsibility for the introduction of the new or improved products and services

■ ensure that a check is carried out on the introduction of the new or improved products and services

■ evaluate the success of the introduction of new or improved products or services and seek to improve it.

83   **Agree plans for the introduction of new or improved products and services to customers**

- ❏ Set the budget(s) for introducing new or improved products or services and agree with relevant stakeholders.

- ❏ Accurately identify any need for specialist support, and the availability of this assistance.

- ❏ Agree with the supplier's specifications and terms regarding the supply of products or components.

- ❏ Accurately calculate profit margins and projections for the time required to recover investment costs.

- ❏ Agree the cost and value of activities and methods with relevant people.

- ❏ Check that schedules for the introduction of new or improved products and services are realistic and take best advantage of market conditions.

- ❏ Agree marketing methods and mix (of price, promotion, product and distribution) both with the relevant stakeholders and with the suppliers chosen to provide marketing services.

- ❏ Confirm the understanding and commitment of staff involved (or likely to be involved) in new or improved products and services, and the plans for their introduction. Make sure all staff are accurately briefed.

Allocate and monitor the introduction of new or improved products and services to customers

84

❏ Identify and agree with appropriate people the staff and departments who will have responsibility for new or improved products and services.

❏ Where appropriate, establish the incentives to be offered to staff for selling new or improved products and services.

❏ Supply all appropriate people with essential information for the introduction of new or improved products and services.

❏ Prepare briefings or training required to enable new or improved products and services to be introduced effectively.

❏ Set realistic targets for the introduction of new or improved products and services, and ensure that these targets take best advantage of market conditions.

❏ Ensure that the systems necessary to record and monitor progress when introducing new or improved products and services are in place and ready for use.

85 Review and improve the introduction of new or improved products and services to customers

❏ Regularly review the level of achievement towards meeting targets for sales, awareness, interest and other marketing goals.

❏ Identify from valid sources of information the reasons why sales, awareness levels and other marketing goals are not achieving targets.

❏ Seek the views of customers in line with organisational policy and mechanisms.

❏ Monitor sales and marketing targets and methods for their effectiveness and level of success.

❏ Obtain, summarise and analyse customer feedback and analysis about new or improved products and services.

❏ Identify, test and employ new or improved sales and marketing methods which will support the introduction of products and services, where necessary.

❏ Present reports and recommendations for changes to product and service introduction clearly and accurately to relevant people.

CHAPTER 8

Managing yourself and others

Improving your own performance

This section is about the ways you can improve your own sales performance.

The checklists will help you to

■ identify development needs and improve your skills

■ be responsible for your own development and manage this with regards to time and resources.

86 Develop your own skills to improve your performance

❏ Assess skills and identify development needs at appropriate intervals.

❏ Confirm that assessments take account of the skills needed to work effectively with all team members.

❏ Ensure that plans for developing skills are consistent with the needs identified.

❏ Check that plans for developing skills contain specific, measurable and realistic objectives.

❏ Undertake development activities that are consistent with plans for developing skills.

❏ Obtain feedback from relevant people and use it to enhance performance in the future.

❏ Update plans for developing skills at appropriate intervals.

- ❑ Assess performance and identify development needs at appropriate intervals.

- ❑ Ensure that assessment is based on current objectives and likely future requirements.

- ❑ Ensure that development assessment takes account of the skills needed to work effectively with other team members.

- ❑ Plan for personal development to be consistent with the needs identified and the resources available.

- ❑ Ensure that plans for personal development contain specific, measurable, realistic and challenging objectives.

- ❑ Obtain support from relevant people to help create learning opportunities.

- ❑ Undertake development activities which are consistent with plans for personal development.

- ❑ Obtain feedback from relevant people and use it to enhance performance in the future.

- ❑ Update plans for personal development at appropriate intervals.

Developing teams

This section is about looking at ways to improve the performance of your team and develop their sales skills.

The checklist will help you to

■ create and execute plans to develop the team and improve their performance.

88 | Develop teams to improve performance

❑ Ensure that development plans are in place and reflect the learning, training and development of all personnel for whom one is responsible.

❑ Incorporate clear, relevant and realistic development objectives.

❑ Clearly identify the process to be used and resources needed.

❑ Confirm that plans are capable of being implemented within the defined timescales.

❑ Identify and check that resources are available to deliver development goals and, if not, acquire resources or revise plans.

❑ Present plans for development in an appropriate and timely manner.

❑ Execute development activities that organise the support team and organisational objectives.

❑ Provide all team members with equal access to relevant development activities.

❑ Demonstrate own commitment to individual and team development through personal support for, and involvement in, the development activities.

❑ Establish across the team a commitment to learning and continuing professional development.

Glossary

allocating work	giving teams and individuals responsibilities for tasks which should achieve agreed work objectives
assessment against development objectives	using various techniques such as tests, observations of performance and discussions to measure members' current skills, knowledge and performance against the agreed objectives for development
assessment of skills	assessment of your skills against your work objectives, personal objectives and the policies and requirements of your organisation
authorised people	team members, colleagues working at the same level as yourself, higher or lower group managers or sponsors, personnel specialists and members of selection teams or boards
benefits	positive results from the use of resources, e.g. improved effectiveness and efficiency is a positive result for the customer
colleagues	those at the same level as you, or at a higher or lower level, either in your organisation or with the organisations for which you have a working relationship
confidentiality	only providing information to those who are authorised to have it
consultation	asking others for their views and involving them openly in decision making
contributions	ideas and information that people want and need to raise in discussions
corrective action	action taken to match actual expenditure to budget such as altering activities, modifying the use of resources or renegotiating the allocation of resources

development activities	any activities undertaken by team members to develop knowledge and skills, such as carrying out work-based projects or assignments, observing expert colleagues at work, reading books and specialist journals, undertaking open learning or computer based training, attending training courses or conferences
digressions	discussions or contributions which deviate or depart from the purpose and objectives of the meeting
ensuring consistency in product or sevice delivery	making sure that the products and services for which you are responsible continuously meet the standards agreed in your organisation and with your customers
equal access	giving every member of your team the same opportunity to be involved in activities or to use resources
evaluation	a balanced assessment of people's work and behaviour
feedback on performance	information you can give to team members on how well they are performing against the objectives which have been agreed
identification of development needs	identification of the gap between the demands of team members jobs, both now and in the foreseeable future, and your current level of performance, knowledge and skills
impact on the environment	the positive or negative effect on the environment that may result from the use of resources
individual inspirations	the personal wishes of individual team members to improve their performance at work, their career prospects or their personal circumstances
individuals	colleagues or team members with whom you work

involving others	gathering other relevant people involved (such as team members, colleagues working at the same level as yourself, higher level managers or sponsors and specialists) to help you, particularly at giving support and feedback, agreeing objectives, deciding on priorities and plans and taking responsibility for the delegated tasks
meetings	coming together with other people to give them information, consult with them or reach decisions
monitoring	keeping a close eye on how resources are used and comparing this with plans or a budget
objectives	clearly define results which you need to achieve that are specific, measurable, agreed with others, realistic and time bound
opportunities	developments, either inside or outside your organisation which could have a positive effect on your work or plans, if you take appropriate action
organisational constraints	your organisation's policies, objectives and level of resources which limit your freedom to take decisions and action
organisational policy	the policies of your organisation relevant to your work activities
organisational policy and procedures	the policies and procedures that affect any information or advice which you may give
personnel	all people working for your organistion; these may be internal or external workers, permanent or temporary, full-time or part-time, paid or voluntary
plan for developing your skills	a plan which identifies your desired level of skills and the activities you are going to undertake in order to reach this level, with a timescale
planning	deciding what to do, when, in what order, and who to get involved; plans may be short term (over the next day, week or month), medium term (over the next few months) or long term (over a year or more)

plans	documents or spoken agreements which describe the work to be carried out when, by whom, to what standard and with what resources, in order that requirements and objectives can be met
policies	rules which govern the use of resources, e.g. planning policies, policies governing the supply of equipment and materials, health and safety policies, environmental policies
prioritisation	deciding the relevant importance and urgency of objectives and tasks, and deciding on which order to tackle them
recipients	the people who receive the information you provide
recommendations	requesting budget allocations or proposing the supply of resources your team needs to achieve its objectives, suggesting new methods of using available resources to improve your team's effectiveness and efficiency
relevant people	team members, colleagues working at the same level as yourself, higher level managers and sponsors, personnel specialists and people outside the organisation
resource constraints	limitations on the amount of time, effort and materials you can give to providing others with information and advice
resources	the time, equipment, materials, services, energy, and premises which you have at your disposal
respect for individuals	the open acknowledgement that individuals have a right to their own views, actions and development as long as these do not unduly constrain the rights of others
reviewing	looking back over what has happened in order to adjust plans (or expectations), if necessary, and learn the lessons from the past
schedules	documents showing the work to be done, when and, sometimes, by whom

standards of work
: the types of behaviour which are acceptable within the working environment, consistent with the values of your organisation, and sometimes described as policies, the quality of work agreed and the way that quality will be measured

style of leadership
: the way you manage the discussions so that a satisfactory result could be achieved

support
: the verbal and actual support (such as giving their time, resources or advice) that is beneficial to you and your activities, and vice versa

systems and procedures for recording and storing information
: the methods that your organisation requires for recording and filing information for future use

team members
: people who work with you as part of a functional project team; team members may report to you either as their line manager or as the manager in charge of a specific project or activity on which they are working

team objectives
: clearly specified results which a team needs to achieve

threats
: developments, inside or outside your organisation, which have the potential to have a negative effect on your work or plans if you do not take appropriate action

trends and developments
: changes in your team, organisation and market; e.g. new skills and working methods, efficiency drives, new products and services, changes in customer requirements

trust
: the feeling held by others that they can believe what you say, that you will act in a consistent way, that you will keep your promises and honour your commitments

values
: the values of your organisation which may be reflected in your organisation's mission, standards of work, relationships between individuals at work, relationships with suppliers, customers and other stakeholders, personnel management and reward systems, training, equal opportunities, health and safety and environmental policies

APPENDIX I

National Standards

What are National Standards?

National standards of performance, or occupational standards, have been developed for virtually all jobs in the UK today. The standards describe what people are expected to do in their jobs and how they are expected to do them. There are occupational standards for retail staff, for cooks, care workers, administrative staff, managers, construction workers and those in the manufacturing and engineering sectors, for instance.

The Sales Standards, developed by the Sales Qualifications Board (SQB), describe the standards of performance expected in sales and sales management. They also describe the knowledge base which salespeople and sales managers need in order to perform effectively. The standards apply to all salespeople and sales managers regardless of the sector in which they are working. While the context may be different, the process of, for example, providing after sales support, processing orders, or delivering product presentations will be similar in all industries.

Organisations and sales personnel in private enterprises use the Sales Standards for a wide range of purposes including recruitment and selection, training needs analysis, designer training programmes, performance review and appraisal, succession planning and promotion criteria. Organisations are now beginning to link them to quality initiatives such as ISO 9000, Total Quality Management and Investors in People.

The Sales Standards, however, like all occupational standards, have been developed for assessment purposes, particularly assessments leading to National Vocational Qualifications (NVQs) or Scottish Vocational Qualifications (SVQs). Sales personnel and sales managers can select units of the Sales Standards which are applicable to their role in order to be assessed for the following qualifications.

- NVQ/SVQ Level 2 in Sales
- NVQ/SVQ Level 3 in Sales
- NVQ/SVQ Level 4 in Sales Management
- NVQ/SVQ Level 4 in Key Account Management
- NVQ/SVQ Level 2 in Telesales
- NVQ/SVQ Level 3 in Telesales

National Vocational Qualifications

National Vocational Qualifications (NVQs), and Scottish Vocational Qualifications (SVQs), are certificates of employees' competence in the job role. They are available to anyone who can prove that they are competent in all the units of the appropriate set of vocational qualifications. There are five levels in the NVQ framework. For example, retail staff can gain VQs in retailing at Levels 1–4, carpenters at Levels 2 or 3 and telesales staff at Level 2 or 3.

Regardless of the sector of the economy in which you are working, you can be awarded an NVQ or SVQ at Levels 2, 3 or 4 in Sales if you can satisfy an assessor that you are competent in the Sales Standards at the appropriate level.

You will usually need to compile a portfolio of evidence supporting your claim to competence, and submit this to an assessor at an approved centre. An NVQ or SVQ is not a training programme. It is a certificate of your competence to do your job as salesperson or sales manager. Of course, you may need some training or development in order to attain that level of competence.

If you are interested in gaining an NVQ or SVQ contact your local approved centre, details of which can be obtained from the Sales Qualifications Board at the Management and Enterprise National Training Organisation.

METO
Russell Square House
10–12 Russell Square
London WC1B 5BZ

Telephone: 020 7872 9000
Fax: 020 7872 9099
Website: www.meto.org.uk

The NVQ Process

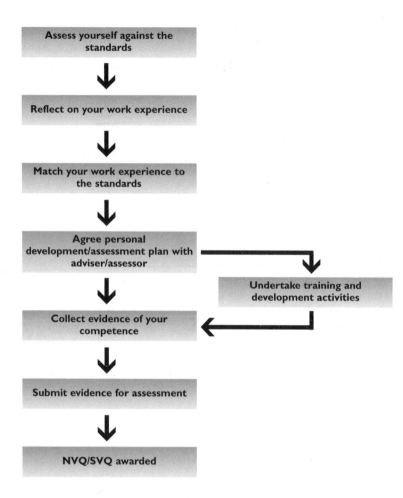

The Sales Standards

The following tables outline the units and elements that make up the Sales Standards. There are six books in total that cover sales, sales management, Key Account management and telesales.

- Sales Level 2
- Sales Level 3
- Sales Management Level 4
- Key Account Management Level 4
- Telesales Level 2
- Telesales Level 3

Sales Level 2

Mandatory units

Unit		Element	
A9	**Continuously improve own sales performance**	A9.1	Monitor and evaluate individual sales calls and own sales performance
		A9.2	Agree and achieve objectives for improving personal sales performance
B31	**Contribute to effective working**	B31.1	Create and maintain professional working relationships
		B31.2	Contribute to effective sales planning
		B31.3	Contribute to the maintenance of health and safety
		B31.4	Maintain the care of resources
C49	**Develop and maintain positive working relationships with customers**	C49.1	Present positive personal image to customer
		C49.2	Balance needs of customer and organisation
		C49.3	Respond to feelings expressed by the customer
		C49.4	Adapt methods of communication to the customer
C52	**Sell products and services to customers in face-to-face settings**	C52.1	Identify the buying needs and interests of customers
		C52.2	Promote the features and benefits of products and services to customers
		C52.3	Help customers to overcome their queries and objections
		C52.4	Agree terms and conditions and close sales
C76	**Contribute to maintaining effective customer service**	C76.1	Maintain quality and customer service standards
		C76.2	Solve problems and customer complaints
		C76.3	Gather feedback to improve service reliability

Sales Level 2

Optional units

Unit		Element	
A10	**Plan and organise a personal work schedule**	A10.1	Plan a personal programme of sales activities
		A10.2	Monitor and evaluate personal work planning
B35	**Input and access data in the organisation's information systems**	B35.1	Maintain an established data storage system
		B35.2	Supply information for a specific purpose
		B35.3	Maintain the confidentiality of information
C41	**Identify sales leads for follow up calls**	C41.1	Identify interest in the organisation's products and services
		C41.2	Agree the nature and time of follow up calls with potential customers
C43	**Follow up and action sales leads**	C43.1	Follow up leads for potential customers
		C43.2	Advise customers of the range and benefits of the organisation's products and services
C60	**Process customers' orders for goods**	C60.1	Confirm the availability of goods to meet customers' requirements
		C60.2	Record and process customers' orders
C61	**Process payments for purchases**	C61.1	Calculate the price of customers' purchases
		C61.2	Process sales payments
C66	**Appraise goods for part exchange**	C66.1	Identify the status and ownership of goods
		C66.2	Assess the condition of the goods for part exchange
C68	**Monitor the delivery of goods to the customer**	C68.1	Prepare for the hand over of goods to the customer
		C68.2	Hand over goods to the customer
C73	**Help customers use products and services**	C73.1	Demonstrate to customers how to use products and services effectively
		C73.2	Support customers during their initial use of products and services
C74	**Meet customers' after sales servicing needs**	C74.1	Arrange after sales support for products and services
		C74.2	Co-ordinate solutions to problems with products and services

Sales Level 3

Mandatory units

Unit		Element	
A6	**Forecast, monitor and evaluate own performance in achieving sales targets**	A6.1	Forecast sales of products and services
		A6.2	Monitor and evaluate the achievement of own sales targets
		A6.3	Analyse sales information and recommend adjustments to sales objectives
A11	**Design, implement and evaluate sales plans**	A11.1	Identify current market trends and conditions
		A11.2	Develop and implement a sales plan to achieve targets
		A11.3	Monitor and evaluate sales plans
B21	**Manage yourself**	B21.1	Develop your own skills to improve your performance
		B21.2	Manage your time to meet your objectives
B28	**Create and maintain effective sales relationships**	B28.1	Identify potential customers, influencers and decision makers within current and potential customers
		B28.2	Develop and enhance positive working relationships with customers
C45	**Generate and follow up sales leads**	C45.1	Make initial contact with potential customers to interest them in products and services
		C45.2	Advise potential customers of the range and benefits of the organisation's products and services
		C45.3	Recognise and exploit opportunities for up-selling and cross-selling
C52	**Sell products and services to customers in face-to-face settings**	C52.1	Identify the buying needs and interests of customers
		C52.2	Promote the features and benefits of products and services to customers
		C52.3	Help customers to overcome their queries and objections
		C52.4	Agree terms and conditions and close sales
C77	**Solve problems on behalf of customers**	C77.1	Identify and interpret problems affecting customers
		C77.2	Take actions to deliver solutions

Sales Level 3

Optional units

Unit		Element	
A1	Contribute to the marketing of products and services	A1.1	Obtain and evaluate information about the market and competitor activity
		A1.2	Make recommendations for the marketing of products and services
B18	Contribute to the development of teams and individuals	B18.1	Contribute to the identification of development needs
		B18.2	Contribute to planning the development of teams and individuals
		B18.3	Contribute to development activities
		B18.4	Contribute to the assessment of people against development objectives
B19	Facilitate individual learning through coaching	B19.1	Coach individual learners
		B19.2	Assist individual learners to apply their learning
B23	Support the efficient use of resources	B23.1	Make recommendations for the use of resources
		B23.2	Contribute to the control of resources
B25	Lead the work of teams and individuals to achieve their objectives	B25.1	Plan the work of teams and individuals
		B25.2	Assess the work of teams and individuals
		B25.3	Provide feedback to teams and individuals on their work
B29	Create effective working relationships	B29.1	Gain the trust and support of colleagues and team members
		B29.2	Gain the trust and support of your manager
		B29.3	Minimise conflict in your team
B32	Maintain activities to meet requirements	B32.1	Maintain work activities to meet requirements
		B32.2	Maintain healthy, safe and productive working conditions
		B32.3	Make recommendations for improvements to work activities
B36	Manage information for action	B36.1	Gather required information
		B36.2	Inform and advise others
		B36.3	Hold meetings

Sales Level 3

Optional units (continued)

Unit		Element	
C38	**Develop, maintain and evaluate (a) customer database(s) for the organisation's products and services**	C38.1	Gather and assess information to create (a) customer database(s)
		C38.2	Create and maintain (a) customer database(s)
C48	**Provide demonstrations of products and services to customers**	C48.1	Prepare for a demonstration of products and services
		C48.2	Demonstrate the features and benefits of products and services to customers
C53	**Negotiate sales**	C53.1	Plan and prepare for sales negotiations
		C53.2	Formulate and make proposals to agree the terms of sale
		C53.3	Negotiate and agree the terms of sale
C55	**Prepare and present proposals and quotations to customers for the supply of products and services**	C55.1	Prepare proposals and quotations for the supply of products and services
		C55.2	Present proposals and quotations for the supply of products and services
C58	**Make sales presentations to existing and potential customers**	C58.1	Prepare for a sales presentation
		C58.2	Give and evaluate a sales presentation
C64	**Assist customers to secure finance for purchases**	C64.1	Identify the customer's finance needs
		C64.2	Agree finance arrangements with the customer to enable them to buy products or services
		C64.3	Process finance applications
C67	**Value goods for part exchange**	C67.1	Identify the status and condition of goods for part exchange
		C67.2	Agree the value of goods for part exchange with customers
C69	**Monitor and finalise the hand over and implementation of products and services**	C69.1	Monitor the delivery and implementation of products and services
		C69.2	Confirm with customers their satisfaction with products and services

Sales Level 3

Optional units (continued)

Unit		Element	
C75	Support the ongoing servicing, maintenance and repair of products and services	C75.1	Arrange for the servicing and maintenance of products and services
		C75.2	Co-ordinate the repair and replacement of products and services
C78	Initiate and evaluate change to improve service to customers	C78.1	Obtain and use feedback from customers
		C78.2	Communicate patterns and trends in customer service within the organisation
		C78.3	Contribute to the evaluation of changes designed to improve service to customers
		C78.4	Initiate changes in response to customer requirements

Sales Management Level 4

Mandatory units

Unit		Element	
A3	Contribute to sales strategy	A3.1	Identify trends, developments and current market conditions
		A3.2	Gather, analyse and evaluate the sales activities of the organisation and its competitors
		A3.3	Contribute to the development and implementation of sales strategy
		A3.4	Recommend changes to improve sales strategy
A8	Forecast sales for products and services	A8.1	Forecast sales of products and services
		A8.2	Monitor, analyse and evaluate the achievement of sales targets
A13	Develop, implement and evaluate sales plans	A13.1	Develop sales plans to achieve targets
		A13.2	Implement sales plans
		A13.3	Gather, analyse and evaluate information on the implementation of sales plans
B22	Develop your own resources	B22.1	Develop yourself to improve your performance
		B22.2	Manage your own time and resources to meet your objectives

Optional units

Unit		Element	
A4	Monitor compliance with quality systems	A4.1	Plan to audit compliance with quality systems
		A4.2	Implement the audit plan
		A4.3	Report on compliance with quality systems
A14	Contribute to project planning and preparation	A14.1	Clarify the project's scope and definition
		A14.2	Provide plans to achieve the project's goals
		A14.3	Contribute to project preparation

Sales Management Level 4

Optional units (continued)

Unit		Element	
A15	Co-ordinate the running of projects	A15.1	Support the project team
		A15.2	Co-ordinate activities, resources and plans
		A15.3	Keep stakeholders informed of project plans
A16	Contribute to project closure	A16.1	Complete project activities
		A16.2	Contribute to the evaluation of project planning and implementation
B17	Select personnel for activities	B17.1	Identify personnel requirements
		B17.2	Select required personnel
B20	Develop teams and individuals to enhance performance	B20.1	Identify the development needs of teams and individuals
		B20.2	Plan the development of teams and individuals
		B20.3	Develop teams to improve performance
		B20.4	Support individual learning and development
		B20.5	Assess the development of teams and individuals
		B20.6	Improve the development of teams and individuals
B24	Manage the use of financial resources	B24.1	Make recommendations for expenditure
		B24.2	Control expenditure against budgets
B26	Manage the performance of teams and individuals	B26.1	Allocate work to teams and individuals
		B26.2	Agree objectives and work plans with teams and individuals
		B26.3	Assess the performance of teams and individuals
		B26.4	Provide feedback to teams and individuals on their performance
B27	Facilitate meetings	B27.1	Lead meetings
		B27.2	Make contributions to meetings
B30	Develop productive working relationships	B30.1	Develop the trust and support of colleagues and team members
		B30.2	Develop the trust and support of your manager
		B30.3	Minimise interpersonal conflict

Sales Management Level 4

Optional units (continued)

Unit		Element	
B33	Manage activities to meet requirements	B33.1	Implement plans to meet customer requirements
		B33.2	Maintain a healthy, safe and productive work environment
		B33.3	Ensure products and services meet quality requirements
B34	Contribute to improvements at work	B34.1	Improve work activities
		B34.2	Recommend improvements to organisational plans
B37	Provide information to support decision making	B37.1	Obtain information for decision making
		B37.2	Record and store information
		B37.3	Analyse information to support decision making
		B37.4	Advise and inform others
C39	Determine the preferred customer base for the organisation's products and services	C39.1	Evaluate the organisation's products and services
		C39.2	Determine the organisation's criteria for selling to customers
		C39.3	Assess the potential for expansion in the existing customer base
		C39.4	Assess the potential for attracting new customers
		C39.5	Develop an overall sales strategy for developing the customer base
C40	Develop, audit and renew networks of current and prospective customers	C40.1	Develop networks across the current and prospective customer base
		C40.2	Audit customer networks to determine opportunities for improvement, expansion and re-orientation
		C40.3	Extend customer networks to provide a base for improved sales
C47	Co-ordinate the introduction of new products and services	C47.1	Agree plans for the introduction of new products and services to customers
		C47.2	Allocate and monitor the introduction of new products and services to customers
		C47.3	Review and improve the introduction of new products and services to customers

Sales Management Level 4

Optional units (continued)

Unit		Element	
C54	Identify and optimise opportunities for the sale of products and services to customers	C54.1	Generate customer interest in products and services
		C54.2	Prepare for and present information to promote the organisation's products and services to Key Account customers
		C54.3	Generate solutions to customer problems and objections
		C54.4	Formulate and make proposals to agree the terms of sale
		C54.5	Negotiate and agree terms and contracts, and close sale
C55	Prepare and present proposals and quotations to customers for the supply of products and services	C55.1	Prepare proposals and quotations for the supply of products and services
		C55.2	Present proposals and quotations for the supply of products and services
C57	Prepare and submit tenders for the supply of products and services	C57.1	Evaluate tender enquiry documentation
		C57.2	Assess the resource requirements and costs of a tender
		C57.3	Finalise and submit a tender application
C59	Lead major sales presentations and promotions	C59.1	Develop and agree the format, content and approach of sales presentations with team members
		C59.2	Present information and arguments on the benefits of using the organisation for the supply of products and services
		C59.3	Evaluate the effectiveness of the sales presentation
C64	Assist customers to secure finance for purchases	C64.1	Identify the customer's finance needs
		C64.2	Agree finance arrangements with the customer to enable them to buy products or services
		C64.3	Process finance applications
C79	Develop and improve service systems	C79.1	Marshal customer feedback from internal and external systems
		C79.2	Modify current service systems in response to customer feedback
		C79.3	Innovate and monitor new service delivery systems
		C79.4	Solve generic customer problems

Key Account Management Level 4

Mandatory units

Unit		Element	
A2	Contribute to the development and implementation of organisational marketing and sales policy and strategy	A2.1	Review and implement organisational marketing and sales policy and strategy
		A2.2	Obtain and evaluate marketing information
		A2.3	Make recommendations for the marketing of products or services
A7	Forecast, monitor and evaluate sales performance of account teams and self	A7.1	Set objectives for personal and account teams sales performance
		A7.2	Plan activities and determine work methods to achieve objectives
		A7.3	Monitor, evaluate and enhance overall sales performance of account teams and self
A12	Design and implement a Key Account Plan	A12.1	Identify customer needs, interests and market activity
		A12.2	Specify a sales plan to achieve Key Account objectives
		A12.3	Implement and evaluate the achievement of the Key Account Plan
B22	Develop your own resources	B22.1	Develop yourself to improve your performance
		B22.2	Manage your own time and resources to meet your objectives
C46	Determine a strategy for the promotion of products and services to Key Accounts	C46.1	Analyse competitor sales activity
		C46.2	Identify trends, developments and current market conditions
		C46.3	Evaluate and determine sales options
		C46.4	Prepare and present a sales strategy to key stakeholders
C50	Establish, maintain and enhance productive working relationships with customers	C50.1	Identify potential customers, influencers and decision makers within current and potential Key Accounts
		C50.2	Develop and enhance productive working relationships with customers, influencers and decision makers
		C50.3	Support Key Account customers in the use of products and services

Key Account Management Level 4

Mandatory units (continued)

Unit	Element	
C54 Identify and optimise opportunities for the sale of products and services to customers	C54.1	Generate customer interest in products and services
	C54.2	Prepare for and present information to promote the organisation's products and services to Key Account customers
	C54.3	Generate solutions to customer problems and objections
	C54.4	Formulate and make proposals to agree the terms of sale
	C54.5	Negotiate and agree terms and contracts, and close sale
C79 Develop and improve service systems	C79.1	Marshal customer feedback from internal and external systems
	C79.2	Modify current service systems in response to customer feedback
	C79.3	Innovate and monitor new service delivery systems
	C79.4	Solve generic customer problems

Optional units

Unit	Element	
B20 Develop teams and individuals to enhance performance	B20.1	Identify the development needs of teams and individuals
	B20.2	Plan the development of teams and individuals
	B20.3	Develop teams to improve performance
	B20.4	Support individual learning and development
	B20.5	Assess the development of teams and individuals
	B20.6	Improve the development of teams and individuals

Key Account Management Level 4

Optional units (continued)

Unit		Element	
B24	Manage the use of financial resources	B24.1	Make recommendations for expenditure
		B24.2	Control expenditure against budgets
B27	Facilitate meetings	B27.1	Lead meetings
		B27.2	Make contributions to meetings
B30	Develop productive working relationships	B30.1	Develop the trust and support of colleagues and team members
		B30.2	Develop the trust and support of your manager
		B30.3	Minimise interpersonal conflict
B33	Manage activities to meet requirements	B33.1	Implement plans to meet customer requirements
		B33.2	Maintain a healthy, safe and productive work environment
		B33.3	Ensure products and services meet quality requirements
B37	Provide information to support decision making	B37.1	Obtain information for decision making
		B37.2	Record and store information
		B37.3	Analyse information to support decision making
		B37.4	Advise and inform others
C39	Determine the preferred customer base for the organisation's products and services	C39.1	Evaluate the organisation's products and services
		C39.2	Determine the organisation's criteria for selling to customers
		C39.3	Assess the potential for expansion in the existing customer base
		C39.4	Assess the potential for attracting new customers
		C39.5	Develop an overall sales strategy for developing the customer base
C40	Develop, audit and renew networks of current and prospective customers	C40.1	Develop networks across the current and prospective customer base
		C40.2	Audit customer networks to determine opportunities for improvement, expansion and re-orientation
		C40.3	Extend customer networks to provide a base for improved sales

Key Account Management Level 4

Optional units (continued)

Unit		Element	
C47	**Co-ordinate the introduction of new products and services**	C47.1	Agree plans for the introduction of new products and services to customers
		C47.2	Allocate and monitor the introduction of new products and services to customers
		C47.3	Review and improve the introduction of new products and services to customers
C55	**Prepare and present proposals and quotations to customers for the supply of products and services**	C55.1	Prepare proposals and quotations for the supply of products and services
		C55.2	Present proposals and quotations for the supply of products and services
C57	**Prepare and submit tenders for the supply of products and services**	C57.1	Evaluate tender enquiry documentation
		C57.2	Assess the resource requirements and costs of a tender
		C57.3	Finalise and submit a tender application
C59	**Lead major sales presentations and promotions**	C59.1	Develop and agree the format, content and approach of sales presentations with team members
		C59.2	Present information and arguments on the benefits of using the organisation for the supply of products and services
		C59.3	Evaluate the effectiveness of the sales presentation
C64	**Assist customers to secure finance for purchases**	C64.1	Identify the customer's finance needs
		C64.2	Agree finance arrangements with the customer to enable them to buy products or services
		C64.3	Process finance applications
C70	**Control and maintain trade**	C70.1	Control the trading process
		C70.2	Monitor the provision of transport
		C70.3	Maintain the trading process
		C70.4	Analyse the trading process and make policy recommendations

Key Account Management Level 4

Optional units (continued)

Unit	Element	
C71 Plan, organise and monitor a distribution system for international trade and services	C71.1	Plan a distribution system for international trade and services
	C71.2	Organise the distribution system for international trade and services
	C71.3	Monitor the distribution system for international trade and services

Telesales Level 2

Mandatory units

Unit		Element	
A9	**Continuously improve own sales performance**	A9.1	Monitor and evaluate individual sales calls and own sales performance
		A9.2	Agree and achieve objectives for improving personal sales performance
B31	**Contribute to effective working**	B31.1	Create and maintain professional working relationships
		B31.2	Contribute to effective sales planning
		B31.3	Contribute to the maintenance of health and safety
		B31.4	Maintain the care of resources
C51	**Sell products and services over the telephone to customers**	C51.1	Develop an effective relationship with the telephone customer
		C51.2	Identify the buying needs and interests of customers
		C51.3	Promote the features and benefits of products and services to customers
		C51.4	Help customers to overcome their queries and objections
		C51.5	Secure the terms of commitment with the customer
C76	**Contribute to maintaining effective customer service**	C76.1	Maintain quality and customer service standards
		C76.2	Solve problems and customer complaints
		C76.3	Gather feedback to improve service reliability

Telesales Level 2

Optional units

Unit		Element	
A10	Plan and organise a personal work schedule	A10.1	Plan a personal programme of sales activities
		A10.2	Monitor and evaluate personal work planning
B35	Input and access data in the organisation's information systems	B35.1	Maintain an established data storage system
		B35.2	Supply information for a specific purpose
		B35.3	Maintain the confidentiality of information
C41	Identify sales leads for follow up calls	C41.1	Identify interest in the organisation's products and services
		C41.2	Agree with potential customers the nature and time of follow up calls from others
C42	Follow up and action telesales leads	C42.1	Follow up leads for potential customers for telesales
		C42.2	Advise customers of the range and benefits of the organisation's products and services
C60	Process customers' orders for goods	C60.1	Confirm the availability of goods to meet customers' requirements
		C60.2	Record and process customers' orders
C72	Support customers in using products and services	C72.1	Explain to customers how to use products and services effectively
		C72.2	Support customers during their initial use of products and services
C74	Meet customers' after sales servicing needs	C74.1	Arrange after sales support for products and services
		C74.2	Co-ordinate solutions to problems with products and services

Telesales Level 3

Mandatory units

Unit		Element	
A5	Forecast, monitor and evaluate own performance in achieving telesales targets	A5.1	Forecast sales of products and services
		A5.2	Monitor and evaluate the achievement of own telesales targets
		A5.3	Analyse sales information and recommend adjustments to sales objectives
A11	Design, implement and evaluate sales plans	A11.1	Identify current market trends and conditions
		A11.2	Develop and implement a sales plan to achieve targets
		A11.3	Monitor and evaluate sales plans
B21	Manage yourself	B21.1	Develop your own skills to improve your performance
		B21.2	Manage your time to meet your objectives
B28	Create and maintain effective sales relationships	B28.1	Identify potential customers, influencers and decision makers within current and potential customers
		B28.2	Develop and enhance positive working relationships with customers
C44	Generate and follow up telesales leads	C44.1	Make initial contact with potential customers to interest them in products and services
		C44.2	Advise potential customers of the range and benefits of the organisation's products and services
		C44.3	Recognise and exploit opportunities for up-selling and cross-selling
C51	Sell products and services over the telephone to customers	C51.1	Develop an effective relationship with the telephone customer
		C51.2	Identify the buying needs and interests of customers
		C51.3	Promote the features and benefits of products and services to customers
		C51.4	Help customers to overcome their queries and objections
		C51.5	Secure the terms of commitment with the customer
C77	Solve problems on behalf of customers	C77.1	Identify and interpret problems affecting customers
		C77.2	Take action to deliver solutions

Telesales Level 3

Optional units

Unit		Element	
A1	Contribute to the marketing of products and services	A1.1	Obtain and evaluate information about the market and competitor activity
		A1.2	Make recommendations for the marketing of products and services
B18	Contribute to the development of teams and individuals	B18.1	Contribute to the identification of development needs
		B18.2	Contribute to planning the development of teams and individuals
		B18.3	Contribute to development activities
		B18.4	Contribute to the assessment of people against development objectives
B19	Facilitate individual learning through coaching	B19.1	Coach individual learners
		B19.2	Assist individual learners to apply their learning
B23	Support the efficient use of resources	B23.1	Make recommendations for the use of resources
		B23.2	Contribute to the control of resources
B25	Lead the work of teams and individuals to achieve their objectives	B25.1	Plan the work of teams and individuals
		B25.2	Assess the work of teams and individuals
		B25.3	Provide feedback to teams and individuals on their work
B29	Create effective working relationships	B29.1	Gain the trust and support of colleagues and team members
		B29.2	Gain the trust and support of your manager
		B29.3	Minimise conflict in your team
B32	Maintain activities to meet requirements	B32.1	Maintain work activities to meet requirements
		B32.2	Maintain healthy, safe and productive working conditions
		B32.3	Make recommendations for improvements to work activities
B36	Manage information for action	B36.1	Gather required information
		B36.2	Inform and advise others
		B36.3	Hold meetings

Telesales Level 3

Optional units (continued)

Unit		Element	
C38	Develop, maintain and evaluate (a) customer database(s) for the organisation's products and services	C38.1	Gather and assess information to create (a) customer database(s)
		C38.2	Create and maintain (a) customer database(s)
C55	Prepare and present proposals and quotations to customers for the supply of products and services	C55.1	Prepare proposals and quotations for the supply of products and services
		C55.2	Present proposals and quotations for the supply of products and services
C62	Control cash and credit transactions	C62.1	Control customer credit
		C62.2	Process customer payments
		C62.3	Reconcile customer accounts
C64	Assist customers to secure finance for purchases	C64.1	Identify the customer's finance needs
		C64.2	Agree finance arrangements with the customer to enable them to buy products or services
		C64.3	Process finance applications
C69	Monitor and finalise the hand over and implementation of products and services	C69.1	Monitor the delivery and implementation of products and services
		C69.2	Confirm with customers their satisfaction with products and services
C75	Support the ongoing servicing, maintenance and repair of products	C75.1	Arrange for the servicing and maintenance of products and services
		C75.2	Co-ordinate the repair and replacement of products and services
C78	Initiate and evaluate change to improve service to customers	C78.1	Obtain and use feedback from customers
		C78.2	Communicate patterns and trends in customer service within the organisation
		C78.3	Contribute to the evaluation of changes designed to improve service to customers
		C78.4	Initiate changes in response to customer requirements

APPENDIX 2

Useful contacts

The following organisations may be useful to contact for further information.

Management and Enterprise National Training Organisation (METO)
Tel: 020 7872 9000

Chartered Institute of Marketing (CIM)
Tel: 01628 427500

Direct Selling Association
Tel: 020 7497 1234

Institute of Professional Sales
Tel: 01628 427372

Institute of Sales and Marketing Management (ISMM)
Tel: 01727 812500

Institute of Sales Promotion (ISP)
Tel: 020 7837 5340

Scottish Qualifications Authority (SQA)
Tel: 0141 248 7900

Qualifications and Curriculum Authority (QCA)
Tel: 020 7509 5555

Index

Please note the index refers to page numbers *not* checklists

Advice
  customers, 12–13, 100
After sales support, 89–102
Analysis
  forecasts, 18
  part exchange, 119
  sales activities, 31
  sales forecasts, 26
  sales performance, 20
  sales strategy, 33
  targets, 30
  tender risks, 61
Assessment
  against development objectives, 142
  expansion potential, 6
  networks, 22
  new customers, 7
  part exchange, 119
  performance, 135
  of skills, 142
  tenders, 60
  trends, 28

Commitment, 90, 138
Communication, 98
  see also feedback
  with customers, 13, 37–45
  patterns and trends, 125
Competitors, 30, 31
Complaints, 96
Conclusion
  project activities, 76
  the sale, 51–3
Confidentiality, 61, 142
Contingency plans, 29
Contracts, 52
Co-ordination
  activities, 73
  plans, 73

  project team, 69–77
  resources, 73
  solutions to problems, 95
Costs, tenders, 60
Credit checks, 112
Cross-selling, 42
Customers
  advice, 12–13, 100
  after sales support, 89–102
  base, 1–13, 21
  communication, 13, 37–45
  delivery, 85–7, 90, 91, 93
  demonstration, 82–4, 92
  feedback, 96–8
  finance, 109–15
  follow up, 45, 64
  goods availability, 84
  goods hand over, 87
  identification, 10
  initial contact, 11
  interest, 43
  key accounts, 63–8
  networks, 21–3
  new or improved services, 128–30
  order processing, 86
  personal image, 41
  presentations, 65–6
  pricing, 106–19
  problems identification, 99
  satisfaction, 91
  service, 125, 126
  solutions to problems, 48, 95,
    100, 102
  support, 35–53, 93
  working relationship, 38

Delivery, 85–7, 90, 91, 93
Demonstration, 81–4, 92
Development, 146

activities, 143
identification, 28
needs, 143
plans, 138
presentations, 65
sales plan, 27
sales strategy, 32

Enquiries
tender documentation, 58
Evaluation, 143
customer feedback, 96, 97
customer service, 126
existing products/services, 4
offer to tender, 57–8
part exchange, 119
potential expansion, 6
presentations, 66, 68
project planning, 77
sales activities, 31
sales calls, 19
sales plans, 29
sales strategy, 33
targets, 30
tender enquiries, 58

Feedback, 4, 96–8, 100, 134
customer satisfaction, 91
marketing, 124
on performance, 143
projects, 71, 72
sales plans, 29
tenders, 61
Financing, 109–15
Follow up, 45, 64, 95
Forecasts, 18, 26

Goods
availability, 84
condition assessment, 119
hand over, 87
payment balance, 110
status and ownership, 118

Implementation
products and services, 90

project planning, 77
sales plans, 27
sales strategy, 32
Improvement
performance, 15–33, 133–5, 138
products and services, 128–30
Individuals
aspirations, 143
definition, 143
Innovation, 101, 127–30

Key Account Management
Level 4, 162–6
Key Accounts, 55, 63–8

Leadership style, 145

Maintenance, 94, 95
Market, 9–13, 28
Marketing effort, 121–30
Management and Enterprise NTO (METO), 149
Monitoring, 144
customer feedback, 96, 97
delivery, 90, 100
new or improved services, 129
sales activities, 31
sales calls, 19
sales plans, 29
service, 101
targets, 30, 130
trends, 28
Motivation, 75

National Standards, 147–71
National Vocational Qualifications (NVQs), 148, 149–50
Negotiation
planning and preparation, 44
terms of sale, 106, 108
Networks, 21–2, 23

Objectives, 144
assessment against development, 142

organisational, 27
performance improvement, 20
projects, 70
sale calls, 19
Order processing, 85–7
Organisation
benefits, 64
constraints, 144
policy, 144
procedures, 144
sales objectives, 27
selling criteria, 5

Part exchange, 117–19
Patterns and trends, 125
Payments, 115
Performance
feedback, 143
improvement, 15–33, 133–5, 138
team development, 138
Personal development, 135
Personal image, 41
Personnel, 144
Planning, 25–33, 144
evaluation, 77
implementation, 77
sales negotiations, 44
Plans, 144
contingency, 29
co-ordination, 73
development, 138
monitor and evaluate, 29
new or improved services, 128
project goals, 72
skill development, 134
targets, 27
Preparation
demonstration, 82
presentations, 66, 67
project, 70
proposals, 113
sales negotiations, 44
Presentations, 79–102
development, 65
evaluation, 68

key accounts, 63–8
organisation's benefits, 64
preparation, 66, 67
proposals, 114
Pricing, 103–19
Processing
orders, 85–7
sales payments, 115
Projects, 55, 69–77
Promotion, 66, 111
Proposals
preparation, 113
presentations, 114
terms of sale, 49, 106

Quotations, 113–14

Recommendations, 33
definition, 145
marketing, 124
Records and documentation
agreements, 52, 53
customers' orders, 86
goods hand over, 87
projects, 76
tenders, 58, 61
Research, 17–23
Resources, 145
constraints, 145
co-ordination, 73
management, 135
requirements, 60
Reviewing, 130, 145

Sales Level 2, 152–3
Sales Level 3, 154–7
Sales Management Level 4, 158–61
Sales Qualification Board (SQB), 148, 149
Sales Standards, 151–71
Scottish Vocational Qualifications (SVQs), 148, 149
Self-management, 131–8
Servicing, 94, 95

Skills
assessment, 142
development, 134
Stakeholders
information, 74
marketing, 128
projects, 71
tenders, 60
Standards, 145, 147–71
Strategy
changes recommendation, 33
customer base development, 8
development & implementation, 32
Support, 146
after sales, 89–102
customers, 35–53, 93
teams, 75

Targets
monitor, analyse & evaluate, 30
new or improved services, 129

review, 130
sales plan, 27
Teams
development, 137–8
members, 146
objectives, 146
presentations development, 65
project, 69–77
support, 75
Telesales Level 2, 167–8
Telesales Level 3, 169–71
Tenders, 55–61
Terms and conditions, 53
Terms of sale, 49, 106, 108, 114
Time management, 135
Trends, 18, 28, 146
Trust, 38, 146

Up-selling, 42

Working relationships, 38